Facilitator's Handbook

Instruction for All Students

Paula Rutherford

Instruction for All Students Facilitator's Handbook

Published by Just ASK Publications & Professional Development
2214 King Street
Alexandria, Virginia 22301
Toll Free 1-800-940-5434
FAX 1-703-535-8502
email info@justaskpublications.com
www.justaskpublications.com

©Copyright 2009 by Just ASK Publications
All Rights Reserved

The Learning Experience Tools may be duplicated for non-commercial use in the purchaser's school or district. The Learning Experiences themselves may not be copied, reproduced, translated or transmitted in any form, electronic or mechanical, including photocopying or any information storage system and retrieval system now known or to be developed. Any other use of these materials requires written permission from Just ASK Publications & Professional Development.

The ***Instruction for All Students Facilitator's Handbook*** CD-ROM includes templates and exemplars for your use. Please see copyright statement included with CD-ROM for duplication rights.

Printed in the United States of America
ISBN 978-0-9797280-2-0
Library of Congress Control Number 2009924019
10 9 8 7 6 5 4 3 2 1

Table of Contents

Collegial Conversations
Build in time at the beginning of each session to hold collegial discussions about how you have used previous learning in your classrooms and professional practice. See page 275 in ***Instruction for All Students*** for questions that can frame these discussions.

Chapter I In the News & Influencing Our Thinking
Learning Experience
I-1: In the News Jigsaw

Chapter II Lesson & Unit Design
Learning Experiences
II-1: Where Are We with Standards-Based Education?
II-2: The Planning Process in a Standards-Based Environment
II-3: Using the Top Ten Questions
II-4: Unit Design in the Standards-Based Classroom
II-5: Concept-Based Instruction
II-6: Task Analysis
II-7: An Awesome Array of Planning Approaches

Tools
Tool II- 1: Self-Assessment: Course and Unit Planning
Tool II- 2: Standards-Based Education - What Elements Are You Using
Tool II- 3: Standards-Based Planning Process
Tool II- 4: Unit Design in the Standards-Based Classroom
Tool II- 5: The Top Ten Questions
Tool II- 6: Task Analysis T-Chart
Tool II- 7: Unit Plan A
Tool II- 8: Unit Plan B
Tool II- 9: Unit Plan C
Tool II-10: Unit Organizer Map
Tool II-11: Multiple Intelligences Unit Map
Tool II-12: Unit Design Brainstorming Map
Tool II-13: Lesson Planning Guide
Tool II-14: Course Map
Tool II-15: Standards-Based Instruction Planning Matrix

Table of Contents

Chapter III Presentation Modes: Updating Old Faithfuls
Learning Experiences
III-1: Framing the Learning
III-2: Demonstrations, Lectures, and Discussions
III-3: Literacy Across the Curriculum (including Technology Literacy)
III-4: Vocabulary Development

Tools
Tool III-1: Self-Assessment: Framing the Learning
Tool III-2: Making Connections
Tool III-3: Updating Old Faithfuls Log

Chapter IV Active Learning
Learning Experiences
IV-1: Beyond Chalk and Talk
IV-2: Repertoire Building Scavenger Hunt

Tools
Tool IV-1: Self-Assessment: Active Learning
Tool IV-2: Stir the Class
Tool IV-3: Active Learning Log
Tool IV-4: Collegial Collaborators

Chapter V Assignments
Learning Experiences
V-1: Self-Assessment
V-2: Let's Go RAFTing
V-3: Homework

Tools
Tool V-1: Self-Assessment: Assignments
Tool V-2: RAFT
Tool V-3: Homework Planning Guide
Tool V-4: Stoplight

Table of Contents

Chapter VI The Assessment Continuum
Learning Experiences
VI-1: Self-Assessment
VI-2: Assessment as a Learning Experience
VI-3: Growth-Producing Feedback
VI-4: Assessment Jigsaw
VI-5: Going from Knowing to Doing

Tools
Tool VI-1: Self-Assessment: Classroom Assessment
Tool VI-2: Assessment Planning Guide
Tool VI-3: Growth-Producing Feedback
Tool VI-4: Assessment Jigsaw

Chapter VII Products & Perspectives
There are no learning experiences for **Chapter VII Products and Perspectives**. The products and perspectives found in this chapter are referenced and used in the learning experiences in other chapters.

Chapter VIII Differentiation of Instruction
Learning Experiences
VIII-1: Getting Started with Differentiation
VIII-2: Introduction to the 3 x 3 Model
VIII-3: Sources, Processes, and Products
VIII-4: Scaffolding Sort
VIII-5: Repertoire Building Jigsaw

Tools
Tool VIII-1: Self-Assessment: Inclusive Instruction
Tool VIII-2: Getting Started with Differentiation
Tool VIII-3: Differentiating Sources, Learning Processes, and Demonstrations of Learning
Tool VIII-4: Scaffolding Sort
Tool VIII-5: Active Learning Strategies through the Lens of Multiple Intelligences Theory

Table of Contents

Chapter IX Thinking Skills for the 21st Century

Learning Experiences
IX-1: Self-Assessment
IX-2: 21st Century Thinking Skills in Action
IX-3: Using Bloom's Taxonomy

Tools
Tool IX-1: Self-Assessment: 21st Century Thinking Skills
Tool IX-2: Thinking Skills for the 21st Century Circles
Tool IX-3: Using Bloom's Taxonomy
Tool IX-4: Williams' Taxonomy

Chapter X The Learning Environment

Learning Experiences
X-1: Self-Assessment: Communicating High Expectations
X-2: Building Student Responsibility
X-3: Space, Time, and Procedures

Tools
Tool X- 1: Self-Assessment: Communicating High Expectations
Tool X- 2: Incomplete Assignment Log
Tool X- 3: Contract for Improvement Points
Tool X- 4: Error Analysis
Tool X- 5: Daily Log
Tool X- 6: Skill Building and Meaning Making
Tool X- 7: Learning Log
Tool X- 8: Reflections on the Week
Tool X- 9: 3-2-1
Tool X-10: Procedure Potpourri

Chapter XI Collegial Collaboration

Learning Experiences
XI-1: Self-Assessment
XI-2: Focus on Data Analysis and Integration
XI-3: Formats for Collegial Conversations
XI-4: Working Together in the Classroom

Table of Contents

Tools
Tool XI-1: Self-Assessment: Collegial Collaboration
Tool XI-2: Item Indicator Analysis
Tool XI-3: Cause and Effect Analysis
Tool XI-4: Data Analysis and Integration
Tool XI-5: Standards-Based Observations I
Tool XI-6: Standards-Based Observations II
Tool XI-7: Peer Observations and Learning Walks
Tool XI-8: Peer Observation Reflections

Appendix: Resources to Support Learning Communities
- ***Instruction for All Students*** CD-ROM Table of Contents
- Standards-Based Unit Exemplars
    Second Grade - Ghana
    Middle School Science - Force and Motion
- Online Resources from Just ASK

Introduction

This facilitator's handbook is designed to help educators structure the reading and use of the strategies presented in *Instruction for All Students*. It can be used for book clubs, study groups, and for team, department, and faculty meetings. The learning experiences are interactive and action-oriented. The handbook is written with the expectation that group participants will use what they read and discuss in one session and come to the next session ready to share and discuss how they used what they learned.

It is not necessary to move through *Instruction for All Students* sequentially. A group might decide to focus on planning first quarter, assessment second quarter, active learning third quarter, and differentiation fourth quarter. It is recommended that all groups engage in the **Learning Experience I-1: In the News Jigsaw** exercise to set the stage for future study and use of the text.

Suggested Formats
- One-hour book club or study group sessions (There are enough learning experiences for at least 24 one-hour sessions.)
- Three-hour sessions on professional development days focused on areas of need and interest
- 30 to 45 minute instructional focus at each faculty meeting
- Hybrid of face-to-face sessions and online discussions for collegial discussions and displays of participant use of strategies in their classrooms
- Overview session to introduce the book:
  - **Learning Experience I-1: In the News Jigsaw** exercise in **Chapter I: In The News** OR
  - **Learning Experience II-3: Using The Top Ten Questions** exercise in **Chapter II: Lesson and Unit Design**

Components of Each Session
- Mutual understanding of the purposes/outcomes of each learning experience
- **Collegial Conversations** about how participants used strategies studied in previous session in their classrooms and professional practice
  - Page 275 in *Instruction for All Students* provides questions to guide these conversations.
  - Sharing of students and teacher work
  - An online or print journal
- Input and processing of new information
- Professional practice expectations articulated

Introduction

Materials and Tools

- Each participant needs a copy of ***Instruction for All Students*** by Paula Rutherford. Books may be ordered from Just ASK Publications:
  - 1-800-940-5434 (voice)
  - 1-703-535-8502 (fax)
  - Online at www.justaskpublications.com
  - Ask about quantity discounts.
- A **CD-ROM of Tools** is attached to the inside back cover of ***Instruction for All Students***. Some of those tools are used in the Learning Experiences outlined in this text. There are, however, additional tools on that CD-ROM.
- Two free e-newsletters are available to support and extend the learning. They are titled ***Mentoring in the 21st Century*** and ***Just for the ASKing!*** You can access these newsletters at www.justaskpublications.com.
- **An Instruction for All Students CD-ROM of Visual Tools** is available from Just ASK Publications for an additional fee. These visual tools can be used to make charts, handouts, and transparencies and can be inserted into PowerPoint and Keynote presentations.
- The following information for setting up study groups can be found in this handbook on page 3 of the Introduction as well as in the Table of Contents.
  - Facilitating Book Clubs and Study Groups
  - A Menu of Learning Experiences for each chapter
  - ***Facilitator's Handbook*** CD-ROM of Tools Table of Contents

Facilitating Book Clubs and Study Groups

Process Facilitator
- For the entire process to function smoothly, a "go-to" person or "Most Responsible Person" (MRP) should be identified.
- This person does not have to do all the preparation work but should be kept in the loop by all individuals regarding plans and any change of plans regarding attendance, meeting times, meeting locations, etc.

Meeting Arrangements
- Number of sessions
- Length of sessions
- Dates of sessions
- Location of sessions
- Refreshments for sessions

Focus Areas
The areas of focus (Chapters) to be studied and the learning experiences to be completed need to be identified.

Materials Preparation
- Materials such as copies of the tools used in the sessions can be prepared for each session or all materials can be prepared in advance.
- All tools are available in this handbook in hard copy and on the CD-ROM.

Session Facilitation
Identify a session facilitator. One person can take responsibility for facilitating all the sessions or the responsibility can be rotated between members of the group.
- The session facilitator is responsible for ensuring that all the logistical matters function smoothly including, as appropriate, the preparation of listed support materials.
- The session facilitator is also responsible for ensuring that the group stays focused on the identified outcomes and that group norms are followed in both face-to-face and online sessions.

Facilitating Book Clubs and Study Groups

Group Norms Established
Variables to consider include:
- Attendance
- Punctuality
- Interactions/communication protocols during and between the sessions
- Decision-making process
- Completion of professional practice assignments

Words of Thanks

The publication of this book was guided by Caitlin Cooper's keen eye, determination to ensure consistency and clarity, and willingness to deal cheerfully with ever-changing deadlines and design specifications. Thanks, Caitlin.

Thanks also goes to Shilpa Shah for her technical support and collaboration with Caitlin in getting this text to press.

In The News
& Influencing Our Thinking

1

In The News Jigsaw

Purposes
- Provide an overview of *Instruction for All Students*
- Help participants
  - Identify the patterns and trends found in the initiatives/areas of focus discussed in the text
  - Make connections between these initiatives/areas of focus and teaching and learning in a standards-based classroom
  - Make connections between what you read and discuss in this exercise and what you are working on in your school

Time
60 to 90 minutes

Materials
- *Instruction for All Students*: Chapter I and other selected pages
  - Pages 2-3 are used to introduce the learning experience
  - Page 5 is used to summarize the learning experience
  - The following pages are used in the Jigsaw learning exercise:
    - **The Learning-Centered Classroom:** pages 6-7, 251
    - **High School Reform:** pages 8-9
    - **21st Century Thinking Skills:** pages 12, 220-221
    - **Literacy across the Curriculum:** pages 15, 79-80
    - **Meeting the Needs of Diverse Learner:** pages 20-21, 199
    - **Technology Integration:** pages 27, 133-134
    - **Assessment as A Learning Experience:** pages 22-24
    - **Looking at Student Work:** pages 283-285
    - **Dealing with Unmet Expectations:** pages 259, 260-261

Process
- Turn to pages 2-3 in *Instruction for All Students* and read the summary of some of the key ideas that shape the contents of the text.
- Discuss with a partner what you find surprising, curious, or interesting.
- Then use the **Jigsaw Classroom** process described on pages 242-243 in *Instruction for All Students* to delve deeply into the initiatives mentioned on pages 2-3.

In The News Jigsaw

- Each member of the study group or each small group within the study group reads a segment(s). The topics and pages are:
  - **The Learning-Centered Classroom:** pages 6-7, 251
  - **High School Reform:** pages 8-9
  - **21st Century Thinking Skills:** pages 12, 220-221
  - **Literacy across the Curriculum:** pages 15, 79-80
  - **Meeting the Needs of Diverse Learners:** pages 20-21, 199
  - **Technology Integration:** pages 27, 133-134
  - **Assessment as A Learning Experience:** pages 22-24
  - **Looking at Student Work:** pages 283-285
  - **Dealing with Unmet Expectations:** pages 259, 260-261
- If two or more people read the same segment, those reading the same selection should meet in expert groups to discuss the key ideas. If only one person is assigned each segment, skip this step.
- Each participant/group of participants presents a brief summary of the key ideas and connections in the assigned segment to the larger group.
- Following the presentation on all of the topics, turn to page 5: **Yesterday and Today** to examine the graphic that captures past practice and current thinking about best practice in a 21st century standards-based classroom.
- Discuss how the information presented in the **Today** column captures the essence of what was studied in the Jigsaw learning exercise.

Professional Practice

- Bring artifacts from your classrooms/offices that represent the **Today** column on page 5: **Yesterday and Today** in each of the three areas: curriculum, instruction, and assessment to the next session. The information studied in the Jigsaw learning exercise provides further guidance about what type of artifacts to collect.
- These artifacts may be either teacher or student work and will be used as exemplars in the opening collegial discussions in the next session.

Lesson & Unit Design

II

Where Are We with Standards-Based Education?

Purposes
- Provide time for collegial conversation about current best practice in the participants' classrooms
- Identify the current realities of participants in their journey from being standards-referenced to being standards-based

Time
- 30 minutes for **Collegial Conversations**
- 30 minutes for **Where Are We with Standards-Based Education (SBE)?**

Materials
- Participants' artifacts for **Yesterday and Today** exercise: See professional practice for Chapter I for details.
- *Instruction for All Students* pages 28-30
- Page 35 or a copy of **Tool II-2: Standards-Based Education: What Elements are You Using?** for each participant

Process
- Spend 30 minutes in groups of 4 to 6 sharing the artifacts you brought to represent the **Today** column on page 5: **Yesterday and Today**.
- Read pages 28-30 in *Instruction for All Students* for the following key ideas related to standards-based education:
  - Standards guide all classroom decisions.
  - The focus is always on student learning.
  - Expectations for learning are the same for all students, even those who have traditionally performed at low levels.
  - The final determination of the effectiveness of instructional practices is whether or not they result in higher levels of achievement for students.
  - Assessment results are used to inform the teacher about the effectiveness of curricular decisions.
- Use the statements on the bottom of half of page 28 to focus a discussion on where you are individually and collectively on the continuum of moving from standards-referenced to standards-based.

Where Are We with Standards-Based Education?

- After that discussion, turn to page 35 or distribute **Tool II-2**: **Standards-Based Education: What Elements Are You Using?**
- Use that tool to do a self-assessment of your current practice.
- Highlight the areas with which you need the most assistance in implementing in your instructional practice.
- Then move around the group asking two or three other people for recommendations about how you can increase your use of the variables you marked: sometimes, seldom, or never.

Professional Practice

- Focus between now and the next session on the variables of SBE planning you identified as areas for growth.
- Note on an index card two or three efforts you make to focus on those variables. Note also the impact of those efforts on your instructional decision making.
- Bring the note cards to the next session.

The Planning Process
in a Standards-Based Environment

Purposes
- Consider big picture planning for the entire school year rather than focusing only on individual lessons
- Identify and practice using the four essential questions in the SBE Planning Process
  - What should students know and be able to do?
  - How will the students and I know when they are successful?
  - What learning experiences will facilitate their success?
  - Based on data, how do I refine the learning experiences?

Time
30 minutes

Materials
- *Instruction for All Students* pages 32-34
- **Self-Assessment: Course and Unit Planning** - Use page 33 or prepare a copy of **Tool II-1: Self Assessment: Course and Unit Planning** for each participant
- A copy of **Tool II-3: SBE Planning Process** for each participant

Process
- Turn to page 33 in *Instruction for All Students* or distribute a copy of **Tool II-1: Self-Assessment: Course and Unit Planning**.
- Complete the self-assessment and then discuss in small groups or with a partner what this assessment revealed about their planning for the year and units.
- Use page 32 as a graphic representation of a year-long planning process.
- Turn to page 34 and read the brief description of the **SBE Planning Process**.
- Distribute copies of **Tool II-3: SBE Planning Process**.
- Analyze a unit or lesson you are teaching right now and fill in the key ideas in each of the four ovals and discuss what you wrote.

Using the Top Ten Questions

Purposes
- Add detail to the **SBE Planning Process Ovals**
- Identify the variables we need to consider when designing lessons or units
- Build skillfulness in using ***Instruction for All Students*** to build repertoire for answering the **Top Ten Questions**

Time
- 30 minutes in multi-session format
- 90 minutes in overview session format

Materials
- ***Instruction for All Students*** pages 36-38 and rest of text for overview
- The **SBE Ovals** participants completed in the previous learning experience: **Overview of the SBE Planning Process**
- A copy of **Tool II-5: Top Ten Questions** for each participant (**Overview Session**)

Process
- Make a list of the questions you consider when you do detailed planning.
- Turn to page 36 in ***Instruction for All Students*** and read the list of the **Top Ten Questions** the author asks herself when she is planning a lesson.
- Engage in a discussion about how these questions align with the questions you ask yourselves.
- Read the boxed information at the top of page 37. The information presented here reveals that the **Top Ten Questions** provide the structure for the rest of the text.
- Pull out the **SBE Ovals** you completed in the last exercise and note how the **Top Ten Questions** relate to the **SBE Ovals**.

Using the Top Ten Questions

Two Hour Overview Session
- Complete **Overview of the SBE Planning Process (II-2)** exercise.
- Complete **Using the Top Ten Questions (II-3)** exercise.
- Distribute copies of **Tool II-5: Top Ten Questions** worksheet.
- Identify a lesson you will be teaching in the near future.
- Work in pairs or small groups to do an overview of ***Instruction for All Students***.
    - Use **Tool II-5: Top Ten Questions** to record information you could use in the identified lesson.
    - Page references are provided on the tool and on pages 37-38 in ***Instruction for All Students***.
    - If you and your partner are teaching the same lesson you can do collaborative planning.
    - If you teach different subjects or grades, do parallel planning and coach each other as you work on your individual lessons.

Unit Design
in the Standards-Based Classroom

Purposes
- Increase understanding of what focused and thorough planning looks like in a standards-based classroom
- Promote planning in units or chunks instead of focusing on daily lesson plans as isolated events

Time
60 minutes

Materials
- *Instruction for All Students* pages 39-42
- A copy of each of the following tools for each participant or notification to participants to access the units on the **Facilitator's Handbook CD-ROM** and bring copies to session
  - **Tool II-4: A Guide to Unit Design in the Standards-Based Classroom**
  - **Standards-Based Unit Exemplar: Second Grade - Ghana**
  - **Standards-Based Unit Exemplar: Middle School Science - Force and Motion**
  - **Tool II-3: SBE-Planning Process**

Process
- Turn to pages 39-42 in *Instruction for All Students* and read through the **Guiding Questions for Unit Design** on those pages noting the **SBE Planning Oval** each set of questions addresses.
- Note the page references for the questions.
- Distribute copies of the standards-based units on **Ghana** (2nd grade) and **Force and Motion** (middle school).
- High school teachers will be amazed by the work the second graders are doing and the level of planning by the teacher.
- Read through the units, note how the unit designers address the **Guiding Questions for Unit Design**, and discuss your findings with colleagues.

Professional Practice
- Distribute copies of **Tool II-3: SBE Planning Process**.
- Focus on an upcoming unit and complete the SBE Planning Ovals using the information you have reviewed and discussed.
- Come to the next session prepared to discuss what you learned from the process and how it was similar to and different from the way you usually plan.

Concept-Based Instruction

Purposes
- Emphasize that memorization of facts is not enough
- Identify the key concepts and big ideas in a course or unit

Time
30 minutes

Materials
Instruction for All Students pages 43-45

Process
- Read page 43 in *Instruction for All Students* and explain to a colleague the relationships between facts, concepts, and generalizations.
- Turn to page 44 and follow the directions at the top of the page.
- Read through the examples of generalizations/essential questions on page 45 and then write two of three generalizations/essential understandings that capture the big ideas of a subject you teach.

Professional Practice
- Review district curriculum documents to determine whether they are fact, concept, or generalization based.
- Bring examples of concept or generalization-based statements you encounter in district documents or in instructional materials to the next session.

The Key to Success
Task Analysis

Purposes
- Determine the role of task analysis in the SBE Planning Process
- Practice task analyzing

Time
60 minutes

Materials
- *Instruction for All Students* pages 46-47, 171-172, 173, and 174
- Two copies of **Tool II-6: Task Analysis T-Chart** for each participant

Process
- Distribute one copy of **Tool II-6: Task Analysis T-Chart**.
- Use one of the **T-Charts** to collaboratively task analyze a common experience appropriate for the group. Possibilities include: planning a wedding, planning a two-week vacation, preparing Thanksgiving dinner for ten, a birthday party for a 7, 10, or 15 year old, etc. Ask participants to list the knowledge and skills they would need to successfully complete the task. The point of the exercise (besides fun) is to point out that we constantly task analyze the projects we undertake.
- Turn to pages 46-47 in *Instruction for All Students* and read the information on task analysis.
- Discuss how task analysis in lesson planning is similar to task analyzing in our personal lives.
- Preview the three performance assessments described on pages 171-172 (high school), 173 (2nd grade), and 174 (middle school).
- Working in pairs, select one of the three performance assessments and complete a task analysis on it. Record your analysis on the second **T-Chart**.
- Hold a whole group discussion about the completed task analyses.

Professional Practice
- Distribute the other copy of **Tool II-6: Task Analysis T-Chart**.
- Complete two task analyses on lessons and/or assessments you use before the next session.
- Bring those task analyses to the next session. Be prepared to discuss how using the task analysis process impacted your instructional decision making.

An Awesome Array of Planning Approaches

Purpose
Explore alternative formats for designing and recording unit and lessons plans

Time
30 minutes

Materials
- *Instruction for All Students* pages 48-54
- Distribute copies or have participants access the following tools on the *Instruction for All Students* CD-ROM (Note: the tool numbers in *Instruction for All Students* may be different than the tool numbers in the *Facilitator's Handbook*):
  - **Tool II- 7: Unit Plan A**
  - **Tool II- 8: Unit Plan B**
  - **Tool II- 9: Unit Plan C**
  - **Tool II-10: Unit Organizer Map** (for student use)
  - **Tool II-11: Multiple Intelligences Unit Map**
  - **Tool II-12: Unit Design Brainstorming Map**
  - **Tool II-13: Lesson Planning Guide**
  - **Tool II-14: Course Map**
  - **Tool II-15: Standards-Based Instruction Planning Matrix**

Process
- Read pages 48-54 in *Instruction for All Students* and, as appropriate, review all of **Chapter II: Lesson and Unit Design**.
- Access the tools listed above and identify the one(s) with the most potential for use in your practice.
- Participate in a small group discussion about which formats would be most useful to you and why.

Professional Practice
- Select at least one of the planning tools and use it to plan a unit or lesson.
- Bring the document to the next session and be prepared to share how it worked and your next steps.

Self-Assessment
Course and Unit Planning

Assess your practice around each of these variables in the planning process.
Almost Always (A), Sometimes (S), Not Yet (N)

Do you...

_____ Frequently review the learning standards for your state and district?

Analyze the curriculum to

_____ examine the guidelines the department, school, district, or state provide?
_____ consider the conceptual themes or big ideas that form the framework for this course?
_____ design essential questions to guide students to an understanding of the key concepts and big ideas?
_____ ask what major thinking skills are used in this course?

Chunk concepts, themes, and skills into units by asking

_____ how concepts and thinking skills can be incorporated into units?
_____ what products and performances could students create/do to demonstrate mastery of these skills and concepts?

Design units around authentic assignments and assessments and

_____ ask yourself how the proposed activities explicitly move the students toward what they should know and be able to do by the completion of the unit?
_____ plan tasks that require the use and analysis of processes important beyond the classroom?
_____ ensure that the tasks are academically rigorous?
_____ plan assignments engaging and relevant enough to motivate students?
_____ orchestrate learning experiences that require the use of a wide variety of thinking skills?
_____ identify specific audiences other than the teacher?
_____ provide precise criteria for assessment of the work known to students prior to the beginning of the work?
_____ check to see that necessary skill building is integrated into meaningful activities rather than being presented as isolated drills?
_____ provide learning experiences that call for in-depth inquiry into concepts cited in the standards and on topics of interest to the students?

What Elements Are You Using?
Standards-Based Education

Give yourself a boost of confidence by taking this quick assessment to identify the elements of Standards-Based Education (SBE) you are currently using.

Curricular materials are selected or developed because they address content standards.

| Never | Seldom | Sometimes | Often | Always |

Instructional strategies are selected or developed that give students opportunities to learn and practice the expectations outlined in the standards.

| Never | Seldom | Sometimes | Often | Always |

What students know and are able to do is clearly defined before a unit of instruction begins.

| Never | Seldom | Sometimes | Often | Always |

Documentation of student learning other than grades is provided to students and parents.

| Never | Seldom | Sometimes | Often | Always |

Students share the responsibility for monitoring their progress toward the standards.

| Never | Seldom | Sometimes | Often | Always |

Student performance on assessment is used to revise and refine the selection of curriculum, instruction, and assessment activities.

| Never | Seldom | Sometimes | Often | Always |

Instruction and assessment are adapted to accommodate students with special needs or alternative learning styles.

| Never | Seldom | Sometimes | Often | Always |

Lesson plans focus on what is to be learned rather than what is to be taught.

| Never | Seldom | Sometimes | Often | Always |

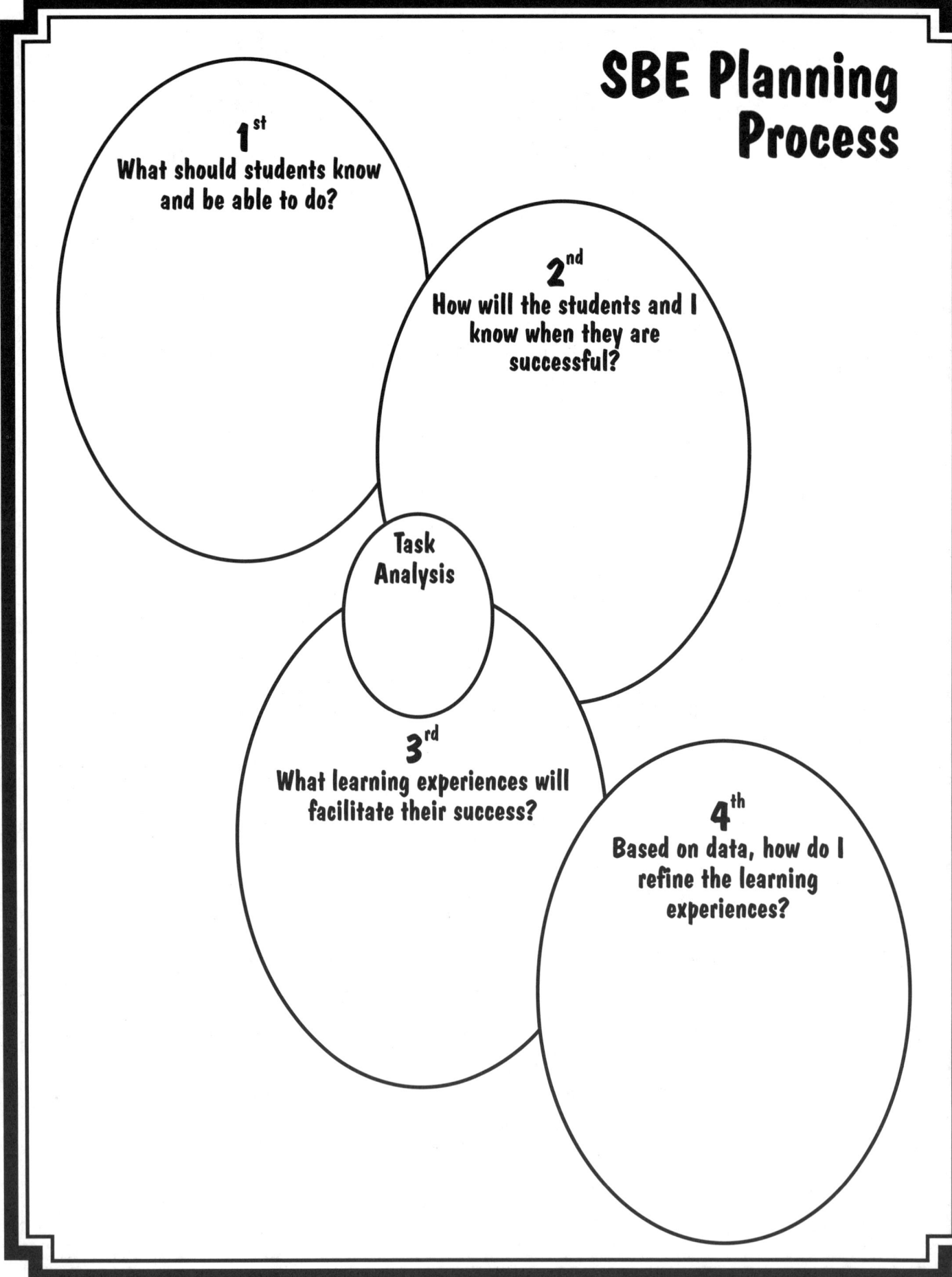

Unit Design in the Standards-Based Classroom

1st Oval: What should students know and be able to do?

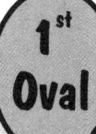

1. On which content standard(s) will the students be working?

2. What are the big ideas, major themes, key concepts, or essential understandings embedded in, or which transcend, the standards listed above? See pages 43-45.

3. Given the essential to know/key concepts and ideas identified in #2 how will this unit be different from what/how I taught and asked students to do in years past? If this is a new unit, skip this question.

Unit Design in the Standards-Based Classroom

4. When and where (inside and outside of school) have the students encountered information about and had experience with these key concepts/big ideas before? Think horizontally and vertically across the curriculum.

2nd Oval: How will the students and I know when they are successful?

5. What would it look like when students can demonstrate that they understand the big ideas and have mastered the essential skills? That is, what are some ways they might demonstrate their capacity to use the newly learned concepts/information appropriately in a new situation? See pages 124-140, 159-174, 176-180.

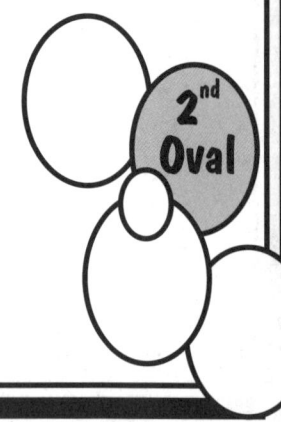

Unit Design in the Standards-Based Classroom

6. Consider the list generated in #5, and determine which tasks/products would best demonstrate student understanding. Decide whether to use a rubric or a performance task list and the criteria to be included. See pages 175-180.

7. What does a task analysis reveal about the skills, the knowledge, and the level of understanding required by the task? See pages 46-47.

8. Do I already have sufficient pre-assessment data or do I need to gather more? If so, what method shall I use? What does the pre-assessment data tell me about the skills and knowledge on which the entire group will need to focus? Are there individual students who will need additional support if they are to have a realistic opportunity to demonstrate mastery? In which areas will they need support? Are there students who would be best served by extensions to the learning experiences? See page 153.

Unit Design in the Standards-Based Classroom

3rd Oval: What learning experiences will facilitate their success?

9. How will I Frame the Learning so that students know what they are going to be doing, what they will know and be able to do as a result of those activities, how they will be assessed, and how everything they are doing is aligned with the standards? See pages 57-61.

10. How will I help students access prior knowledge and use it productively, either building on it or reframing their thinking as appropriate? See pages 88-116.

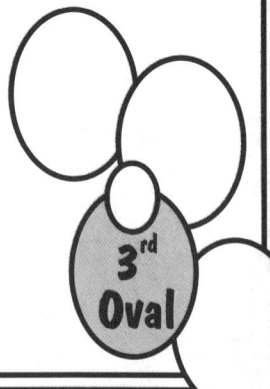

Unit Design in the Standards-Based Classroom

11. What methods of presentation and what active learning experiences can I use to help students achieve the standard? Could I provide multiple sources of information and exercises which would help all students make real-world connections and use rigorous thinking skills? See pages 12-19, 63-82, 157-158, 219-248.

12. What assignments, projects, and homework will help students see the relevance of the learning and help them not only meet the standard but retain their learning? How might I provide multiple pathways to learning? See pages 123-148, 201-216.

13. What are the ways I can gather formative assessment data that will provide me and my students information on their progress toward meeting the standard? See pages 22-25, 154-155.

Unit Design in the Standards-Based Classroom

14. What materials and resources do I need to locate and organize to provide multiple pathways to learning? How should I organize the classroom and the materials to provide easy student access? See pages 202-203, 251-266.

15. What else might I do to provide challenging and meaningful experiences for both struggling and advanced learners? Are there other human, print, or electronic resources I might consult to refine/review my plan? See pages 12-13, 26-27, 133-134, 197-216.

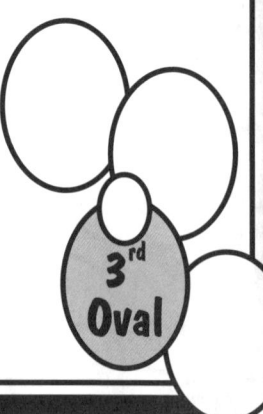

Unit Design in the Standards-Based Classroom

4th Oval: Based on data, how do I refine the learning experiences and/or the assessment?

16. How did students do on the performance task? Were there some students who were not successful? What might account for that? What might I do differently next time? See pages 273, 283-285.

17. What else do I need to consider in my advance planning the next time I am focusing on this standard?

Unit Design in the Standards-Based Classroom

18. Did all of the activities guide students toward mastery of the standard? Are there activities that need to be added, modified, or eliminated? Am I using these activities because I have always used them, or have I analyzed them to be sure that they are the most effective and efficient tools at my disposal?

19. Over all, was this unit effective for addressing the standard(s)? Are there other standards that I could incorporate into this unit or are there other units of study where I can have the students revisit these standards or essential understandings?

TOP TEN QUESTIONS
to ask myself as I design lessons

1st Oval

1. What should **students know and be able to do** as a result of this lesson? How are these objectives related to national, state, and/or district standards? How are these objectives related to the **big ideas/key concepts** of the course? Consult your state and district learning standards and your district curriculum for guidance with this question. See pages 43-45 for information on big ideas and key concepts.

2nd Oval

2. How will **students demonstrate what they know and what they can do**? What will be the **assessment criteria** and what form will it take? See pages 149-181.

TOP TEN QUESTIONS

3rd Oval: Questions 3 - 10 address the 3rd Oval.

3. How will I find out what students already know (**pre-assessment**), and how will I help them access what they know and have experienced both inside and outside the classroom? How will I help them **build on prior experiences**, **deal with misconceptions**, and reframe their thinking when appropriate? See pages 57-61.

4. How will new knowledge, concepts, and skills be introduced? Given the **diversity of my students** and the **task analysis**, what are my **best options for sources and presentation modes**? See pages 55-82.

TOP TEN QUESTIONS

5. How will **I facilitate student processing** (**meaning making**) of new information or processes? What key questions, activities, and assignments (in class or homework) will promote understanding, retention, and transfer? See pages 122-148.

6. What shall I use as **formative assessments** or **checks for understanding** during the lesson? How can I use the **data** from those assessments to **inform my teaching decisions**? See pages 154-156, 283-285.

7. What do I need to do to **scaffold and extend instruction** so that the learning experiences are productive for all students? What are the multiple ways students can access information and then process and demonstrate their learning? See pages 195-216.

TOP TEN QUESTIONS

8. How will I **Frame the Learning** so that students know the objectives, the rationale for the objectives and activities, the directions and procedures, as well as the assessment criteria at the beginning of the learning process? See pages 57-61 and 123.

9. How will I build in opportunities for students to make **real-world connections** and to learn and use the **rigorous and complex thinking skills** they need to succeed in the classroom and the world beyond? See pages 135-140, 180-194 and 217-247.

10. What adjustments need to be made in the **learning environment** so that we can work and learn efficiently during this study? See pages 249-266.

TOP TEN QUESTIONS
to ask myself as I design lessons

Materials to be Gathered or Prepared

Time Line/Sequence for Lesson

Task Analysis

Knowledge | **Skills**

Knowledge | **Skills**

Unit Plan A

Unit of Study

Standards

Essential Questions/Big Ideas/Key Concepts

Assessment Strategies

    Pre-assessment:

    Formative:

    Summative: (What criteria?)

Possible Learning Experiences/Assignments

Materials and Resources Needed

Unit Plan B

Unit Title	Grade/Subject
Standards to be Addressed	**Key Concepts and Generalizations/ Essential Questions**
Summative Assessment	**Task Analysis of Knowledge, Skills, and Levels of Understanding Required**

Map of the Unit Sequence of Events/Lessons	Time Allocation

Materials and Resources	**Technology Resources**
Vocabulary	**Differentiation Strategies (Scaffolding and Extensions)**
Instructional Strategies	**Formative Assessment Strategies**

Tool II-8

Unit Plan C

Unit Title

Time Frame

Standards: What will students know and be able to do as a result of this unit? What are the essential understandings, key concepts, and big ideas?

Assessments: Performance tasks, projects, quizzes, tests, observations, work, samples, etc. How will the students and I know when they are successful?

Task Analysis: What knowledge and skills are needed for success? Which students will need extra help and which students will need enrichment? How will I scaffold instruction?

Instruction: What learning experiences will help students learn targeted understandings?

Unit Organizer Map for:

Previous Unit: Current Unit: Next Unit:

Standard(s)/Benchmark(s)
Restated as a question, "Can I...?"

Relevance - How will I use this knowledge and these skills right now? How are knowledge and skills used by adults?

Assessment(s) - How will I show my teacher I've met/exceeded these standards/benchmarks?

Instruction - What study strategies and resources will I use to help me perform well on the assessment(s)?

This unit is about - What is the main concept, theme, or big idea?

By / By / By / By / By / By / By

© Just ASK Publications

Multiple Intelligences Unit Map

Possible learning experiences for each intelligence:

Logical/Mathematical	Linguistic/Verbal	Bodily/Kinesthetic	Naturalist

Visual/Spatial	Musical/Rhythmic	Intrapersonal	Interpersonal

Standards, Benchmarks, or Indicators to be Addressed
_____
_____
_____

Key Concepts, Big Ideas, Essential Understandings
_____
_____
_____
_____
_____

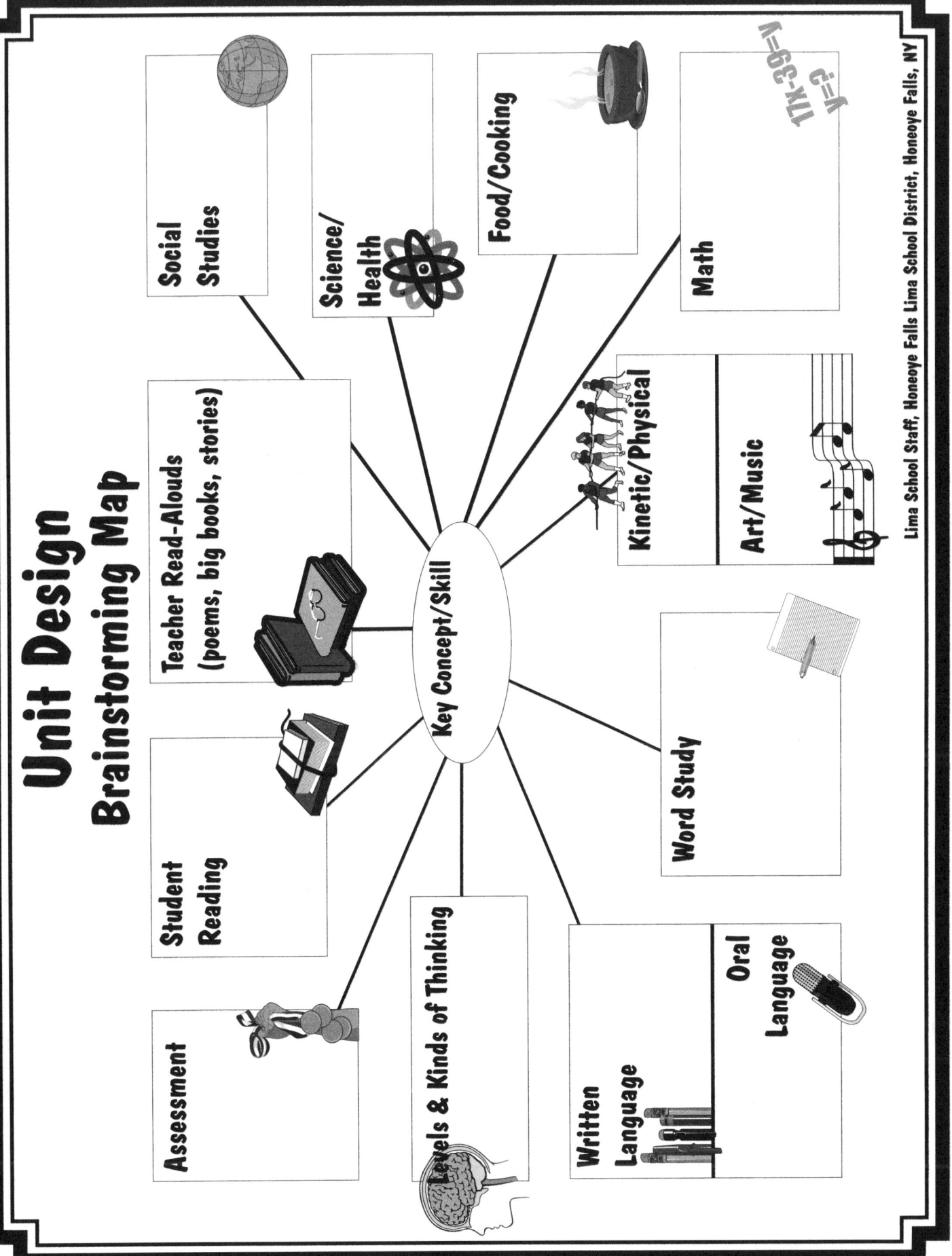

Lesson Planning Guide

Unit

Date(s)

Standard and/or indicators addressed
1.

2.

3.

Standards in kid-friendly language
1.

2.

3.

Concepts, generalizations, or essential questions
1.

2.

3.

Ways to assess students' level of learning during and at the end of the lesson
Formative:
1.

2.

3

Summative:
1.

2.

Lesson Planning Guide

Ways to access prior knowledge and help students make real-life connections
1.

2.

Learning Experiences
1.

2.

3.

4.

5.

6.

Materials and resources needed
1.

2.

3.

Ways to scaffold instruction
1.

2.

3.

Ways to have students summarize
1.

2.

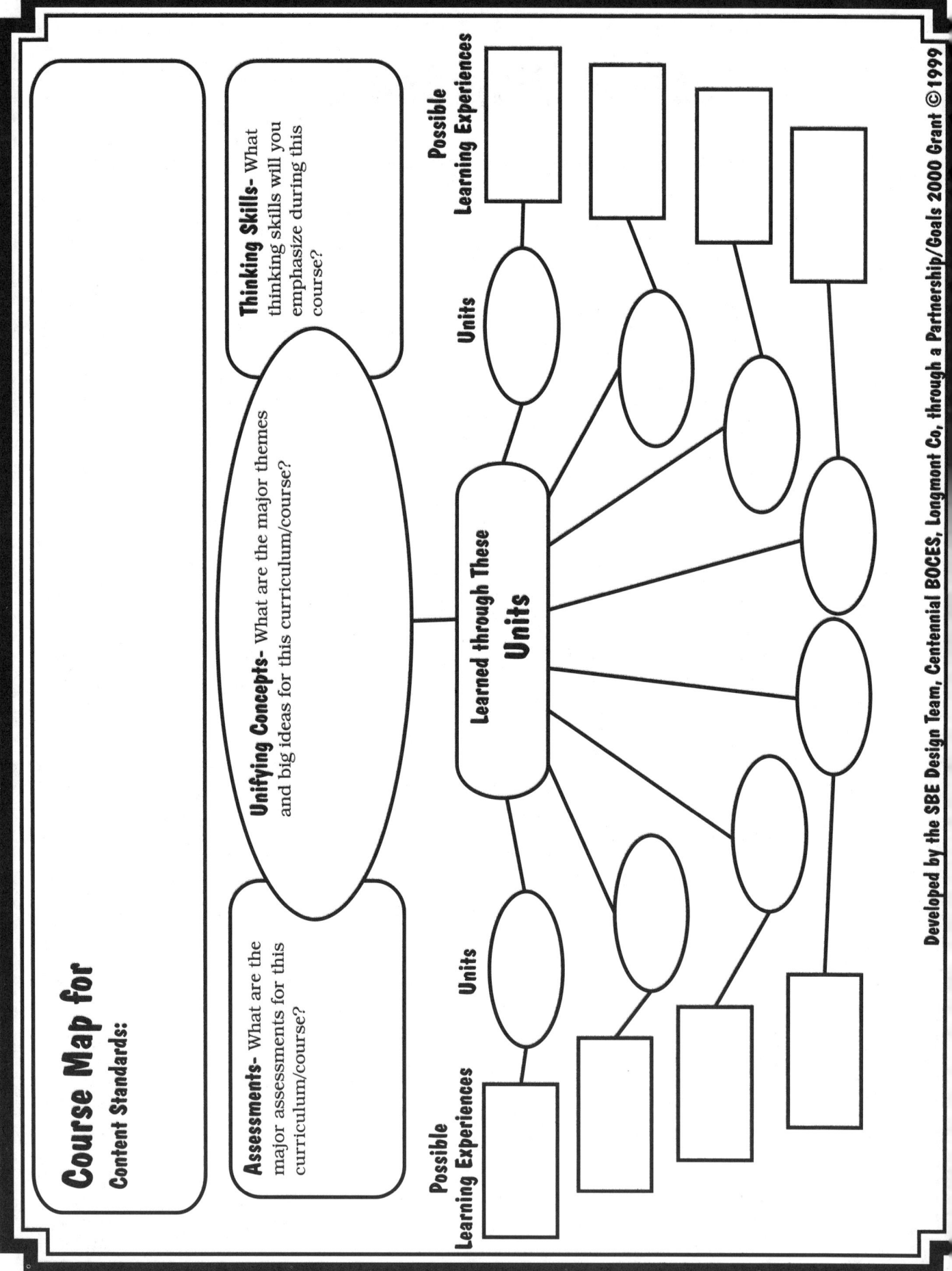

Standards-Based Instruction Planning/Analysis Matrix

Standard	Assignment #1	Assignment #2	Assignment #3	Assignment #4	Traditional Assessment	Performance Assessment
Indicator #1						
Indicator #2						
Indicator #3						
Indicator #4						
Indicator #5						
Indicator #6						
Indicator #7						
Indicator #8						

Use this matrix to analyze current units or to plan future units. Cross reference each component of the unit with subsets of the standards to ensure a high correlation. Make necessary adjustments before, during, and after instruction.

© Just ASK Publications Tool II-15 *Instruction for All Students Facilitator's Handbook*

Presentation Modes
Updating Old Faithfuls

III

Framing the Learning

Collegial Conversations
Build in time at the beginning of each session to hold collegial discussions about how you have used previous learning in your classrooms and professional practice. See page 275 in **Instruction for All Students** for questions to frame these discussions.

Framing the Learning

Purposes
- Explore the power of providing students a framework for learning
- Examine practice around helping students make connections and process learning in ways that promote retention and transfer

Time
30 minutes

Materials
- **Instruction for All Students** pages 56-61
- **Self Assessment: Framing the Learning** on page 57 or a copy of **Tool III-1: Self Assessment: Framing the Learning** for each participant
- A copy of **Tool III-2: Making Connections** for each participant

Process
- Turn to page 57 in **Instruction for All Students** or distribute **Tool III-1: Self-Assessment: Framing the Learning**.
- Complete the self-assessment and then discuss the results with a partner or in small groups.
- Read pages 58-62.
- Distribute copies of **Tool III-2: Making Connections**.
- Complete the analysis and reflection on **Tool III-2: Making Connections**.
- Discuss your reflections with a small group or with a partner.
- The group will return to this focus when you study **Chapter IV: Active Learning**.

Demonstrations, Lectures, and Discussions

Purposes
- Affirm the value and ongoing use of traditional presentation modes
- Explore ways to update those traditional presentation modes so that their use incorporates current best thinking and research about learning theory

Time
- 60 minutes
- This session can be a 30 minute component of a session if the reading is done prior to the session. If reading is done outside of the session, all would read pages 63-64, half would read pages 65-72, and the other half would read pages 73-77.

Materials
- *Instruction for All Students* pages 63-77
- A copy of **Tool III-3: Updating Old Faithfuls Log** for each participant

Process
- Work in small groups or with partners for three minutes to brainstorm a list of the ways you present new information to students.
- After you have generated these lists create a group list. Note those that would fall into the category: **Old Faithfuls**. Likely candidates are lecture, discussion, demonstration, printed text, and various older formats of audio-visuals such as videos and overhead transparencies.
- Distribute the **Updating Old Faithfuls Log**.
- Read pages 63-64 in *Instruction for All Students* which focus on demonstrations and think alouds.
- Participate in partner discussions about the similarities and differences, the pros and cons of the two approaches, and your own experience with each.
- Record the suggestions and strategies you want to remember and use in your instructional practice on the **Updating Old Faithfuls Log**.
- Continue working with your partner. Have one person in the partnership read pages 65-72 on lectures and the other read the pages 73-77 on discussions. Record the key ideas on your **Updating Old Faithfuls Log**.
- Upon the conclusion of your individual reading, share the key points of the section you read with your discussion partner. Record key ideas on your log.

Demonstrations, Lectures, and Discussions

Professional Practice

Select one of the **Old Faithfuls**: demonstration, think alouds, lectures, or discussions. Concentrate on refining your use of that approach between now and the next session. Come to that session prepared to share what you tried and what you learned in the process.

Literacy across the Curriculum

Purposes
- Validate and refine instructional decisions related to embedding literacy instruction across the curriculum
- Examine the practices of accomplished readers and unsuccessful readers and strategies for helping unsuccessful readers be more successful
- Consider the use of journals and interactive notebooks to process learning
- Better help students understand text through the use of graphic organizers and Reciprocal Teaching
- Consider options for embedding technology literacy into instruction

Time
60 minutes

Materials
- *Instruction for All Students* pages 14-15, 78-80, 228-230
- A copy of **Tool III-3: Updating Old Faithfuls Log** for each participant (also used in **III-2: Demonstrations, Lectures, and Discussions**)

Process
- First focus on technology literacy in your classrooms and share in small groups or pairs how you have students use technology to access information and process learning.
- Read pages 26-27, 81-82, 133-134 and 248 in *Instruction for All Students* on technology integration and discuss how what you read matches your current practice. Record key ideas on the **Updating Old Faithfuls Log**.
- You have a choice of readings on literacy across the curriculum. Once you select the segment you want to read, read it and then explain the key points to your colleagues who read different selections.
- The reading selections are:
  - **Profiles of Proficient and Unsuccessful Readers**: pages 15 and 79-80
  - **Reciprocal Teaching and Text Organizational Patterns**: pages 78 and 229-230
  - **The Use of Journals and Interactive Notebooks**: pages 14 and 228
- Record key ideas on the **Updating Old Faithfuls Log**.
- Review your **Updating Old Faithfuls Log**, and respond in writing to the stem: "As a result of what we read and discussed today, I need to..."

Literacy across the Curriculum

Professional Practice

Take the action you wrote in response to the summary stem: "As a result of what we read and discussed today, I need to..." Come to the next session prepared to share what you tried and its impact on student learning.

Vocabulary Development

Purposes
- Build a repertoire of research-based strategies for vocabulary instruction
- Practice selecting the appropriate strategy for identified content and learners

Time
30 minutes

Materials
Instruction for All Students pages 16-19

Process
- Identify ten vocabulary words related to a current unit of study.
- Read pages 16-19 in *Instruction for All Students*.
- To process your reading, select one or more of the formats for vocabulary development described on those pages and design tools to use with your students in the study of the selected words. Format choices are:
  - **Word Splash**
  - **Word Walls**
  - **Frayer Model**
  - **Word Sorts**
  - **Three-Column Charts**
  - **Graphic Organizers**
  - **Inside-Outside Circles (Kagan)**
  - **Six-Step Process (Marzano)**

Professional Practice
Use the selected vocabulary strategies with your students and be prepared to share the results, complete with artifacts, at the next session.

Self-Assessment
Framing the Learning

Assess your practice around each of these research-based strategies for structuring the learning environment in ways that help students process, retain, and transfer their learning.

Almost Always (A), Sometimes (S), Not Yet (N)

At the Beginning of the Lesson: Making Connections

_____ I explicitly communicate the learning outcomes, the relationship of the learning experiences to the outcomes, the assessment, and the assessment criteria before we begin the lesson.

_____ I help students recall what they know about the topic to be studied and/or where they have used or learned related information.

_____ I have students make predictions about the content and give rationales for their predictions.

_____ I work with students to set purposes for study and to generate questions to be answered during the lesson.

During the Presentation of New Information

_____ I pause to have students process/summarize at meaningful points. (I practice **10:2 Theory**.)

_____ We assess old predictions, make new predictions, and/or identify significant information at the processing points.

_____ I help students relate new information to prior knowledge.

_____ I use visuals, manipulatives, props, and realia to provide nonlinguistic representations.

_____ We collaboratively generate more questions throughout the lesson.

At the Close of the Lesson: Locking In the Learning

_____ I facilitate student processing/summarizing of the whole lesson.

_____ We evaluate predictions and use new learning to re-frame thinking.

_____ I ask students to note similarities and differences between the new material and what they already know.

_____ We return to the purposes set for study to see if they were accomplished and identify additional information that would be interesting or helpful.

Making Connections

How do I/how might I help students access what they know and have experienced both inside and outside the classroom that relates to what we are about to read/study?

How do I/how might I help them not only build on prior experiences but re-frame their thinking when appropriate?

To Past Experiences

To Future Experiences

What are the "beyond the classroom" applications/implications of what we are about to read/study? How do I incorporate them into the learning experiences?

How do I/how might I engage students in processing and using new learning in ways that promote retention and transfer?

Between Learning Experiences in the Present

Updating Old Faithfuls Log

Demonstrations	Think Alouds
Lectures	Discussions
Printed Text	Technology Literacy

Active Learning

IV

Beyond Chalk and Talk!

Collegial Conversations
Build in time at the beginning of each session to hold collegial discussions about how you have used previous learning in your classrooms and professional practice. See page 275 in *Instruction for All Students* for questions that can frame these discussions.

Purposes
- Review the research and establish a rationale for including active, meaningful learning in all lessons
- Experience a few active learning strategies and consider how you might use them in your instructional practice

Time
60 minutes

Materials
- *Instruction for All Students* pages 83-120
- **Self-Assessment: Active Learning** on page 85 or a copy of **Tool IV-1: Self-Assessment: Active Learning** for each participant
- A copy of **Tool IV-4: Collegial Collaborators** for each participant
- A copy of **Tool IV-2: Stir the Class** for each participant

Process
- Complete **Self-Assessment: Active Learning** on page 85 in *Instruction for All Students* or distribute copies of **Tool IV-I: Self-Assessment: Active Learning**.
- Discuss with a colleague or in small groups what you learned about your practice by completing the self-assesment.
- Do a survey of the group to see which items were most often missing in action or caused the greatest concern; discuss the causes and effects of those patterns.
- Turn to page 7 and read how active, meaningful learning is one of the four research-based variables of the brain-compatible classroom. This is the first of several pages of research that supports the use of active, meaningful learning.

Beyond Chalk and Talk!

- Read page 86 and engage in a discussion about how the Ebbinghaus and Spitzer research matches your own experiences as learners.
- Read page 87 and page 264 to learn or review the information on Mary Budd Rowe's research on **10:2 Theory** and **Wait Time** and then discuss how this research matches your practice and your experience as learners.
- Distribute **Tool IV-4: Collegial Collaborators** and have participants complete the clock using the directions on page 99. If the group is small skip this exercise.
- There are several versions of this **Learning Buddy** structure on the *Instruction for All Students* **CD-ROM**. Have participants access them either during this session or before the next session.
- Meet with a designated **Collegial Collaborator** or other partner in small groups to discuss how you use or could use such a structure in your instructional program.
- Bring your **Collegial Collaborator Clocks** to each session.
- Turn to page 112 and read about **Think-Pair Share**; then discuss how this strategy incorporates all you have just read about active, meaningful learning.
- Distribute **Tool IV-2: Stir the Class**.
- Turn to page 106 to read the directions for using **Stir the Class**.
- Participate in a **Stir the Class** exercise. Select the stem/area of focus based on the age of the grade level or content area best matched to the participants. See suggestions on page 106 in *Instruction for All Students*.
- Process **Stir the Class** for classroom applications.

Professional Practice

- Use at least one of the following in your instructional practice before the next session:
    - **10:2 Theory**
    - **Wait Time I and II**
    - **Learning Buddies** (see *Instruction for All Students* CD-ROM for content-specific formats)
    - **Stir the Class**
    - **Think-Pair-Share**
- Bring any artifacts (teacher work or student work) they collect to use as exemplars during your **Collegial Conversations** at the next session.

Repertoire Building Scavenger Hunt

Purposes
Build and purposefully use an extensive repertoire of instructional strategies that helps students
- access prior knowledge of content and skills
- surface misconceptions and naïve understandings
- make connections and personal meaning
- increase retention and transfer of their learning

Time
60 minutes

Materials
- *Instruction for All Students* pages 90-119
- Before the session use index cards to create a set o**f Instruction for All Students Strategy Cards**. For groups larger than 25, make two sets of cards. The structures and pages numbers to be written on the index cards follow the directions for this exercise.
- A copy of **Tool IV-3: Active Learning Log** for each participant

Process
- Provide each participant a strategy card with the name of an active learning strategy plus a page number from *Instruction for All Students*. See list of strategies and page numbers on the next page. If your group used **Beyond Chalk and Talk!(IV-1)** you may want to omit **Learning Buddies**, **Stir the Class**, and **Think-Pair-Share** as those strategies were used in that session. Also distribute **Tool IV-3: Active Learning Log**
- Study the strategy listed on the strategy card you are given and become an "expert" on it.
- Record the name and page number of the strategy on your **Active Learning Log**. Add notes about how you might use the strategy and why you think it would be useful in that way.
- When you have completed your "expert entry" circulate throughout the room exchanging information with colleagues.
- Complete an entry for each strategy you discuss so that you can reflect on your current use of each strategy and/or add each to your repertoire.
- After the first round of sharing, you may share either the strategy you studied or one that you learned from a colleague.

Repertoire Building Scavenger Hunt

Professional Practice
- Select one of the strategies that you studied in this session and use it in your classroom/professional development sessions before the next session.
- Write a brief summary using the stems found on page 275 in **Instruction for All Students**.
- Read pages of **Chapter IV: Active Learning** to learn about strategies that you did not discuss during this session. Select three more active learning strategies to read about and be prepared to share your ideas for using the strategies you selected with colleagues.

Active Learning Strategies

Place the name of a strategy and the page number(s) for that strategy on an index card. Make duplicate sets as necessary to match number of participants.

ABC to XYZ 119
All Hands on Deck 96
Anticipation/Reaction Guide 110
Connection Collections 118
Corners (Kagan) 90
Exclusion Brainstorming 108
Facts and Folklore 109
Five Card Draw 97
Frame of Reference 91
Graffiti 92
I Have the Question, Who Has the Answer? 95
Inside-Outside Circles (Kagan) 93
Learning Buddies 99-100
Line-Ups (Kagan) 101-102
Numbered Heads Together (Kagan) 103
Personal Opinion Guide 111
Scavenger Hunt 104-105
Sort Cards 94
Stir the Class 106
Take a Stand 107
Think-Pair-Share 112
Three-Column Charts 113
3-2-1 114
Tic-Tac-Toe 98
Ticket to Leave 115
Walking Tour 116-117

Self-Assessment
Active Learning

Assess your practice around each of these strategies for engaging students in rigorous and relevant active learning.

Almost Always (A), Sometimes (S), Not Yet (N)

_____ 1. I encourage students to express varied opinions as long as they support those opinions with data.

_____ 2. I encourage students to think about how the information they are learning relates to other subjects and their lives beyond the school day.

_____ 3. My students think critically and creatively because I ask questions that have more than one answer.

_____ 4. I encourage students to think and discuss answers with a partner or a small group before answering in the larger group.

_____ 5. I encourage my students to reflect on their experiences when learning something new and they often "mess with" new ideas before lectures or reading.

_____ 6. I help students examine their own thinking and build on their ideas.

_____ 7. I ask students what they already know about a unit before introducing it.

_____ 8. I use essential questions and key concepts to help students organize new information in ways that make sense to them.

_____ 9. Students share responsibility for generating their own vocabulary lists and the questions they want answered.

_____ 10. Students resolve their differences by discussing their thinking.

_____ 11. Class time spent on practice exercises and learning the facts leads to meaningful use of the skills and facts in the near future.

_____ 12. I encourage students to try solving difficult problems, even before they learn all the material.

_____ 13. Students are allowed to explore topics that excite or interest them.

_____ 14. I design assessments around real world applications.

_____ 15. Students help determine how they demonstrate learning and how they are assessed.

**Adapted from *The Student Constructivism and Active Learning Environments Scale*
(The S.C.A.L.E.) by Bonk & Medury, 1991**

Stir the Class on:

1 Your own idea

2 Your own idea

✸ **3** Your own really original idea!

4

5

6

7

8

9

10

11

12

13

14

15

16

17

18

19

20

Active Learning Strategy	How I Might Use This Strategy	Why It Might Be Useful Here

Collegial Collaborators

Assignments

V

Self-Assessment

Collegial Conversations
Build in time at the beginning of each session to hold collegial discussions about how you have used previous learning in your classrooms and professional practice. See page 275 in ***Instruction for All Students*** for questions that can frame these discussions.

Self-Assessment

Purposes
- Access prior knowledge
- Establish purpose for readying and study

Time
15 minutes

Materials
- ***Instruction for All Students*** page 123
- A copy of **Tool V-1: Self Assessment: Assignments** for each participant
- Index cards or small pieces of paper

Process
- Turn to page 122 in ***Instruction for All Students*** and note that questions 5 and 9 are the two **Top Ten Questions** highlighted in **Chapter V: Assignments**.
- Turn to page 123 or distribute copies of **Tool V-1: Self Assessment: Assignments**.
- Complete the self-assessment.
- When you have completed the self-assessment, list the three variables at which you are the most consistent and skillful on one side of an index card and list on the other side the three variables on which your practice needs some fine tuning.
- Meet with a partner to discuss what you wrote about your current practice in designing and giving assignments.

Let's Go RAFTing

Purposes
- Expand repertoire of strategies for creating relevance by helping students make real connections
- Promote student examination of information from a variety of perspectives

Time
30 minutes

Materials
- *Instruction for All Students* pages 135-140, 173, 222-223, and 181-194
- A copy of **Tool V-2: RAFT** for each participant

Process
- Read page 135 in *Instruction for All Students* and then work with a partner to analyze the four short **RAFTs** displayed there. Identify the Role, the Audience, the Format (Product), and the Time/Topic in each example.
- When you have completed the analysis of the **RAFTs** on page 135, examine the **RAFTs** on pages 136-139. Discuss why assignments in this format would be engaging for students.
- Turn to page 140 or distribute copies of **Tool V-2: RAFT**.
- Think of a standard, outcome, or key concept you will be addressing during the next week and then begin to design one or more **RAFTs** for that content.
- For suggestions about roles, formats, and audiences turn to **Chapter VII: Products and Perspectives**. On pages 183-188 you will find a lengthy list of products you could have students create. Pages 189-194 contain an extensive list of roles and audiences that can be built into **RAFTs**.
- Work for 10 to 15 minutes on creating a **RAFT** that you can use during the next week.
- When the work time is over, share one of the **RAFTs** you have created.

Professional Practice
Use one of the **RAFTs** created in the session and bring artifacts (student and/or teacher work) to represent that use to the next session.

Homework

Purposes
- Identify the four categories of homework and practice designing homework using those four categories
- Analyze current practice in assigning homework and the homework problems we face
- Identify changes in instructional practice that have the potential to minimize problems with homework completion and to maximize the learning that results from homework

Time
- 30 minutes
- This session/segment could be completed as **Professional Practice** with a 15 minute follow-up **Collegial Conversation** session.

Materials
- *Instruction for All Students* pages 141-148
- A copy of **Tool V-3: Homework Planning Guide** for each participant
- A copy of **Tool V-4: Stoplight** for each participant

Process
- Turn to a neighbor and describe how your homework procedures are working or not working.
- Distribute the copies of **Tool V-4: Stoplight**.
- Read pages 141-148 in *Instruction for All Students*. As you read, record practices you need to **Stop Doing**, **Keep Doing, and Start Doing**.
- When you have finished the reading and recording discuss with a small group or a partner what you wrote and why.

Professional Practice
- Distribute copies of **Tool V-3: Homework Planning Guide**.
- Identify a subject/area of focus for which you will be giving homework assignments during the next week.
- Redesign those homework assignments using Lee and Pruitt's four categories: Practice, Extension, Preparation, and Creative.
- Use what you wrote on **Tool V-4: Stoplight** to monitor your professional practice around homework and be prepared to engage in discussion about what you learned as a result of this focus.

Self-Assessment
Assignments

Assess your practice around each of these variables to ensure that the assignments you design are a good use of time and energy for you and your students.

Almost Always (A), Sometimes (S), Not Yet (N)

_____ I provide a clear explanation of the task so that students know exactly what they are supposed to do. To double check my clarity, I complete the task following the directions exactly as they are written.

_____ I provide the specific purpose for the task so that students know why they are engaged in the project or assignment.

_____ I explain the relation of the assignment or project to the learning outcomes, standards, key concepts, and essential understandings that provide the focus for our work.

_____ I clearly articulate the relevance of this assignment to life beyond the classroom.

_____ I consider who might be an audience (beyond my inbox) and have students complete the work with that audience in mind.

_____ I know and communicate to students the levels and kinds of thinking required by the task.

_____ I consider how to build student choice into the task and include choice as often as possible.

_____ I am purposeful in the selection and communication of the working conditions for student learning. That is:
- Individual and group work is identified.
- Roles are assigned as appropriate.
- Materials, resources, and equipment are identified and readily available to students.
- Administrative constraints are planned and communicated: time line, order of tasks, how to obtain help and answers to questions, etc.

_____ I task analyze so that I know who has the prerequisite skills and knowledge to successfully complete the task and then build background knowledge and provide scaffolding to those who do not have the needed skills and knowledge.

_____ I communicate exactly how students will know when they have successfully completed the task.

_____ I provide models of and/or practice with new behaviors, processes, and products.

_____ I ensure that students know what to do when they are finished with the assignment or project.

Building Your Own RAFT

Role _____
Audience _____
Form (product) _____
Time _____

Role _____
Audience _____
Form (product) _____
Time _____

Role _____
Audience _____
Form (product) _____
Time _____

Homework Planning Guide

As you plan a unit of study, use the homework categories below to thoughtfully design homework that will help your students move toward mastery of the standards on which the unit is based and will also give you good formative assessment data.

📖 **Practice**

💻 **Preparation**

☎ **Extension**

✉ **Creative**

What language could you use to communicate the homework assignments in a way that students know what to do, know why they are doing it, and know when they are successful?

© Just ASK Publications   Tool V-3   *Instruction for All Students Facilitator's Handbook*

In order to maximize the completion of and learning from homework, I need to...

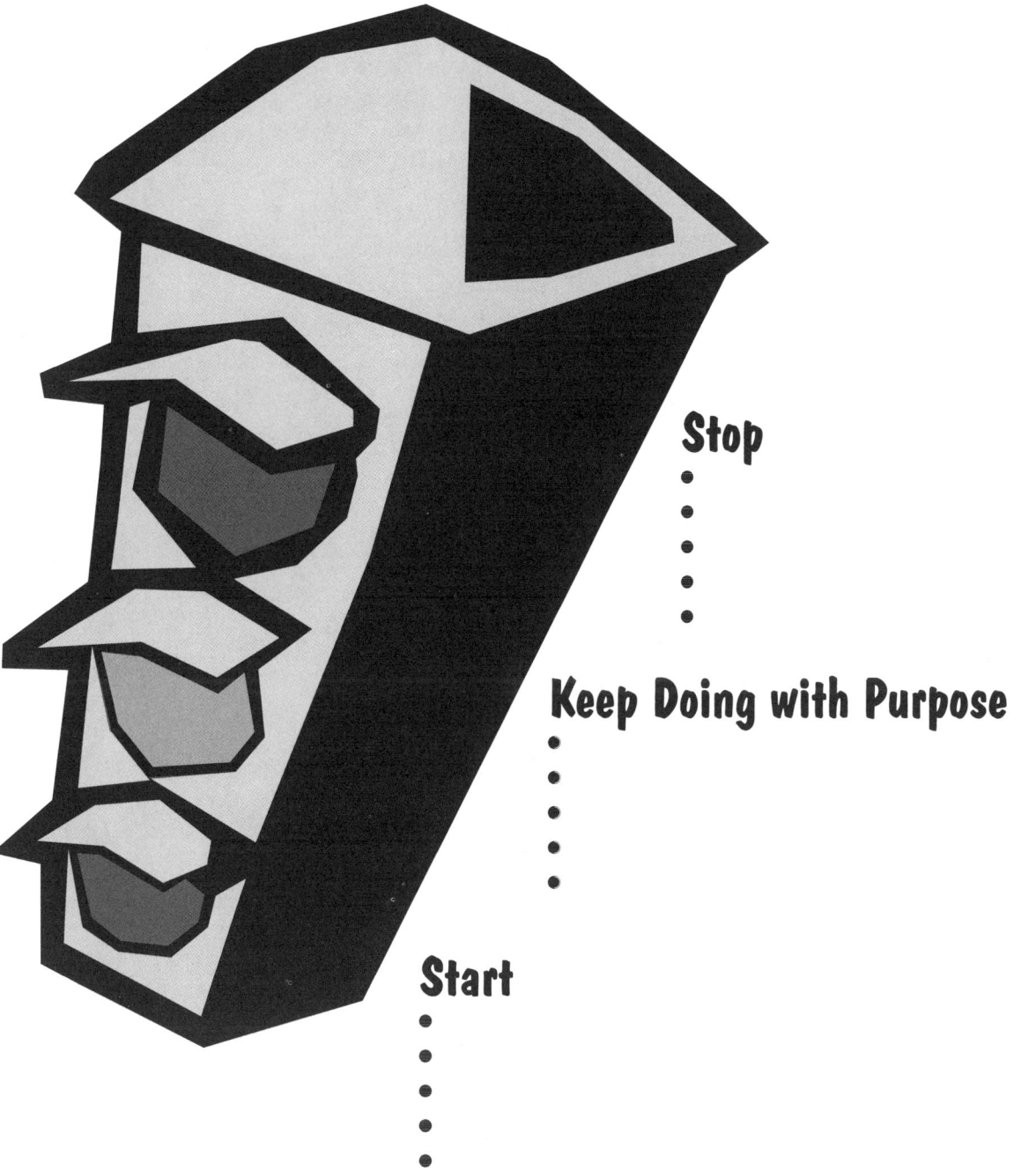

Stop
. . . . .

Keep Doing with Purpose
. . . . .

Start
. . . . .

The Assessment Continuum

VI

Self-Assessment

Collegial Conversations

Build in time at the beginning of each session to engage in collegial discussions about how you have used previous learning in your classrooms and professional practice. See page 275 in *Instruction for All Students* for questions to use in framing these conversations.

Self-Assessment

Purposes
- Identify ten researched-based assessment best practices
- Examine current practice around classroom assessment

Time
15 minutes

Materials
- *Instruction for All Students* page 151
- A copy of **Tool VI-1: Self-Assessment: Classroom Assessment** for each participant

Process
- Turn to page 151 in *Instruction for All Students* or distribute copies of **Tool VI-1: Self-Assessment: Classroom Assessment**.
- Complete the self-assessment marking each item: Almost Always, Sometimes, or Not Yet.
- Engage in a discussion about what you learned about best practice in assessment and how your own practice is aligned with these practices.

Assessment as a Learning Experience

Purposes
- Take an in-depth look at how to use formative assessment to inform practice and improve learning
- Identify specific actions to take to increase the impact of formative assessment

Time
30 minutes

Materials
Instruction for All Students pages 22-24, 159-161

Process
- Review pages 22-24 in **Instruction for All Students** and select two practices that are areas of strength and two that would be areas of growth for you as an educator.
- Discuss in small groups or partnerships the variables you selected and why.
- Following that discussion, turn to pages 159-161 and read through each of the eleven unique formative assessment strategies explained there.
- Identify the one that has the most potential for your own instructional practice.
- Explain to a colleague why you selected this strategy.
- While this task may appear challenging for Pre-K or kindergarten teachers, several of the strategies can be adapted to oral rather than written responses.

Professional Practice
- Monitor your use of practices that can make assessment a learning experience, especially the two you identified as areas for growth in either the self-assessment or the variables listed on pages 22-24.
- Use the selected formative assessment strategy and be prepared to share what you and the students learned from that experience.

Growth-Producing Feedback

Purposes
- Explore the effect grades and comments we make to students have on their learning
- Build capacity in providing growth-producing feedback that positively impacts student learning

Time
45 minutes

Materials
- *Instruction for All Students* page 25
- A copy of **Tool VI-3: Growth-Producing Feedback** for each participant

Process
- After **Collegial Conversations** are completed, discuss how the grades you received in college helped you learn the content being assessed.
- Turn to page 25 in *Instruction for All Students* and read an excerpt of the October 2006 ***Just for the ASKing!*** written by Bruce Oliver.
- After reading, engage in discussion with colleagues about their reactions to what is written there.
- Distribute **Tool VI-3: Growth-Producing Feedback**.
- Analyze the statements listed on those two pages and identify which ones would provide the most helpful feedback to students.
- As time allows, revise the statements that do not provide growth-producing feedback so that they do so.

Professional Practice
- Monitor the feedback you give students between now and the next session and bring three examples of growth-producing feedback you gave students to the next session.
- Be prepared to share examples of ways you provided students opportunities to learn from the feedback they received.
- Access and read the February 2008 issue of ***Just for the ASKing!*** titled: **It's a Feedback World** at www.justaskpublications.com. In this issue Bruce compares growth-producing feedback with Global Positioning Systems (GPS).

Assessment Jigsaw

Purposes
- Expand and refine knowledge base about the wide range of assessment strategies found on the **Assessment Continuum**
- Engage in conversations about how the various assessment strategies are used in instructional practice

Time
- Preparation: 15 minutes
- Collegial Sharing: 45 minutes

Materials
- *Instruction for All Students* pages 149-180
- A copy of **Tool VI-4: Assessment Jigsaw** for each participant

Process
- After **Collegial Conversations** are completed, provide each participant with a copy of **Tool VI-4: Assessment Jigsaw**.
- Follow the directions on **Tool VI-4: Assessment Jigsaw**.

Professional Practice
Review the sections of **Chapter VI: The Assessment Continuum** that you did not read as "the expert" and be prepared to share **one "aha" and one question** at the next session.

Going from Knowing to Doing

Purposes
- Use the wide range of assessment strategies included in the **Assessment Continuum** in the design of a unit
- Experience formative assessment as ongoing and embedded in instruction as you design these assessments

Time
60 minutes

Materials
- *Instruction for All Students* pages 149-180
- A copy of **Tool VI-2: Assessment Planning Guide** for each participant

Process
- Following **Collegial Conversations**, distribute a copy of **Tool VI-2: Assessment Planning Guide** to each participant.
- Work collaboratively with a partner to use all the formats of assessment presented on the **Assessment Continuum** (page 152 in *Instruction for All Students*) in the design of an upcoming extended lesson or unit of study.

Professional Practice
Use the assessments you designed in your instructional practice. Share in the next session what you learned about assessment and its impact on instructional decision making and student learning.

Self-Assessment
Classroom Assessment

Consider whether or not these statements represent your own professional practice.
A (Almost Always), S (Sometimes), N (Not Yet)

_____ I design summative assessments prior to planning the learning experiences for my students.

_____ I use pre-assessments to determine the knowledge, skillfulness, and depth of understanding of the class and individuals about upcoming areas of study and use that data to plan lessons and units.

_____ I task analyze so that I know the component skills and knowledge as well as the level of thinking required by each of the learning experiences and assessments I design/select for my students.

_____ I communicate precise assessment criteria and provide exemplars prior to students beginning the task.

_____ I use classwork and homework as well as student questions and answers in class discussions as formative assessment data and make instructional decisions based on that data.

_____ I use the patterns and trends in the body of assessment data I gather to inform my practice and to evaluate the effectiveness of the instructional decisions I made.

_____ I provide growth-producing feedback to students so that they know how their work is matched to the intended outcome and they know the next steps they need to take.

_____ I collaborate with other teachers to develop, use, and analyze common assessments so that we can identify best instructional practices and areas of our instructional programs that need modification.

_____ I use assessment tools and items that are matched not only to the standards but to the amount of time and emphasis placed on the material during instruction.

_____ I select assessment tools from a wide range of options including, but not limited to, paper and pencil assessments.

Assessment Planning Guide

Lesson/Unit Focus: Date:

How will I use the following assessment strategies in this study?

Pre-assessments:

Checks for Understanding:

Observations/Anecdotal Records:

Student Questions/Comments (In-class and in Journals):

Teacher Questions and Prompts (In-class):

Assignments including Homework (Student Work Samples):

Peer Assessment:

Self-Assessment:

Quizzes:

Tests:

Performance Tasks (Short and Long-Term):

What form(s) will the assessment criteria take?

_____**Analytical Rubric**

_____**Holistic Rubric**

_____**Performance Assessment Task List**

_____**Checklist**

Growth-Producing Feedback?

Analyze the following statements and determine which statements would help students be more successful. Consider how you could revise any that do not appear to be growth-producing so that they are more effective.

- Take a look at the example on the board. Look at my second step and compare it to what you have done.

- I'm not sure you studied very long or hard on this test. I expected better results from you.

- There are just too many careless errors here. Take your paper back and correct your mistakes.

- Your subject/verb agreement is incorrect on numbers 3, 7, and 10. Please go back and fix them and bring your paper back to me.

- Your writing lacks clarity and focus.

- Remember that our objective was to make all your letters touch the line. Go back to your seat and fix the letters that don't follow that pattern.

- You must follow the steps in the recipe precisely. Go back over the steps in the recipe and see if you can find out which step you missed.

- It's clear from your explanation that you have grasped the main ideas. I would recommend one change. Think about your third statement and see if you can make a better argument for your thesis statement.

- In number four, you are dividing fractions. Remember to invert the fraction and then multiply.

- Look at the footnote format I gave you at the beginning of the assignment and see if you can fix the footnotes you have included in your paper.

- I feel that I have presented this information in a clear cut manner. I've done my part. Now you figure out why you aren't getting it.

- Your work is showing great improvement. You're doing much better.

- C+

- Don't make the same mistakes you made the last time. Look at section two of the handout and compare it to your work. I think you'll see where you can make the proper adjustment.

- You will find all of the correct answers in the review sheet I gave you on Friday. Compare your answers with the review sheet, make the necessary corrections, and resubmit your paper.

Growth-Producing Feedback?

- Great work! You are becoming an excellent student.

- I want you to listen to the tape again. Listen to how the narrator pronounces his words. Then come back and try your recitation with me again.

- Look at your materials list and make sure you have included everything that is required for this project.

- You have set up your formula to solve the problem correctly but you made a slight error in step # 2.

- There is no excuse for the kind of work you turned in.

- Let's review. Your paragraph was to have a thesis statement, three supporting statements, and a concluding sentence for a total of five sentences. Here's the paragraph you submitted. I want you to rewrite it correctly.

- You've set up your experiment properly following all the steps in the procedure section of your book.

- Your book report was just superb this time. I enjoyed reading it so much. Great work!

- I'm going to listen to each of you play individually. I want you to do a self-assessment and then I will critique your playing.

- Too vague.

- Your writing has all five components of a good newspaper lead. Keep up the good work.

- This is well done. It's obvious that you took a lot of time to complete your project.

    You did not sound very good today. I hope you improve before next week's concert.

- I explained that to the whole class yesterday. There's no reason why I should have to explain it to you again.

- Remember... *i* before *e* except after *c*. Using this rule, go back and correct your spelling words.

- I want you to do two things. First, go up to the physical model I shared with the class. Then, using this tool, I want you to put the finishing touches on your project so that it looks like the model.

An Assessment Jigsaw

1's: Pre-Assessment and Task Analysis
46-47, 153+, and 88

2's: Checking for Understanding and Questioning
154-156, 157-158, 228, 231-239

3's: Peer and Self-Assessment
14, 162-163, 226-227, 254-255

4's: Homework
141-148

5's: Classroom Test Design
159-161, 165-167, 210

6's: Performance Assessment
168-174, 206-207, 215-216, 222-223

Directions
- Read your assigned section and make notes of key points you would like to discuss when you meet with colleagues who read different sections. If the group is large enough for multiple people to read the same section, those who read the same section will want to spend a few minutes together agreeing on the key points to share with the larger group.
- When you present the key points; be sure to include the following components your presentation:
  - Access prior knowledge
  - Ensure that learners are making connections to their own practice
  - Check for understanding
  - An opportunity for your colleagues to discuss the implications for their practice

Differentiation of Instruction

VIII

Getting Started with Differentiation

Collegial Conversations
Build in time at the beginning of each session for collegial discussions about how you used previous learning in your classrooms and professional practice. See page 275 in ***Instruction for All Students*** for questions that can frame these discussions.

Getting Started with Differentiation

Purposes
- Access and validate prior knowledge and establish a purpose for studying differentiation
- Establish a philosophical approach to thinking about meeting the needs of diverse learners

Time
60 minutes

Materials
- ***Instruction for All Students*** pages 21-22 and pages 197-199
- **Self-Assessment: Inclusive Instruction** on page 197 or a copy of **Tool VIII-1: Self-Assessment: Inclusive Instruction** for each participant
- A copy of **Tool VIII-2: Getting Started with Differentiation** for each participant

Process
- Read pages 21-22 in ***Instruction for All Students*** for background information.
- Complete the **Self-Assessment: Inclusive Instruction** on page 197 or distribute copies of **Tool VIII-1: Self-Assessment: Inclusive Instruction**.
- Discuss the results of your self-assessments with a colleague.
- Be sure to include a discussion about the fact that the same mind set is recommended for advanced and struggling learners.
- Distribute **Tool VIII-2: Getting Started with Differentiation**.
- Use your current knowledge to answer the questions on this planning sheet.
- Talk with a neighbor about any questions or concerns you have as you answer the questions.

Getting Started with Differentiation

- Read page 198 and discuss how the descriptors listed there match your reality. List any other descriptors you would add to the list.
- Given the descriptors of successful and struggling learners on page 198, consider the **Differentiation Non-Negotiables** and actions to take listed on page 199. These general descriptions of actions to take are a good fit for Tier One Response to Intervention (RtI).
- Discuss your own practices around the listed actions to take.

Differentiating Instruction 3 x 3

In addition to a brief introduction to the **3 x 3** model, there are three exercises based on that model. They are:
- **Differentiating Sources, Processes, and Products (VIII-3)**
- **Scaffolding Sort (VIII-4)**
- **Repertoire Building Jigsaw: Readiness, Interests, and Information Processing Styles (VIII-5)**

Build in time at the beginning of each session to discuss your use of the strategies studied in the previous session. Additional time for those conversations should be added to the time cited in each of the exercises described below.

Introduction to the 3 x 3 Model

Purposes
Introduce a graphical representation of differentiation that teachers can reference in planning instruction

Time
10 minutes

Materials
Instruction for All Students page 200

Process
- Turn to page 200 in *Instruction for All Students* and note that the **3 x 3** graphic on that page captures the variables included in the **Differentiation Non-Negotiables** on page 199 and that the framework on pages 199-200 provides the structure for the study of this chapter.
- Read through the three big ideas in each of the three boxes and make your own connections to pages 199-200. Consider how the graphic communicates the key variables we need to consider in the design of differentiated standards-based learning experiences and assessments.
- Focus on the middle box and then discuss the balance of whole-class, small-group, and individual teaching and learning in your instructional program. It is important to note that individual work does not refer to "seat work" but to one-on-one interactions/work with the teacher. If you discover that there is not a balance of the three approaches in all classrooms, engage in a discussion of why that is so and what it would take to achieve such a balance.

Introduction to the 3 x 3 Model

- Next focus on the top box. A differentiated instructional program includes purposeful student choice and variety in the ways that students access information, process their learning, and demonstrate that learning. The next two learning exercises are designed to help you build repertoire with ways to do that.
- Focus on the bottom box and note three significant variables listed there: **Readiness, Interests, and Information Processing Styles**. These are the variables that influence decisions about grouping, sources of new information, processing opportunities, and demonstrations of learning. You will engage in two exercises to expand and refine your repertoires and skillfulness with addressing readiness, interests, and information processing styles.

Differentiating Sources, Processes, and Products

Purpose
Identify resources in *Instruction for All Students* to use in providing multiple pathways to learning

Time
45 minutes

Materials
- *Instruction for All Students*
- A copy of **Tool VIII-3: Differentiating Sources, Learning Processes, and Demonstrations of Learning** for each participant

Process
- The focus for this exercise is the top box on the **Differentiating Instruction 3 x 3** graphic found on page 200 in *Instruction for All Students*.
- Identify a unit or extended lesson you will be teaching in the near future that you would like to differentiate.
- Distribute copies of **Tool VIII-3: Differentiating Sources, Learning Processes, and Demonstrations of Learning**.
- Access the page references for *Instruction for All Students* listed at the bottom of each column to make lists of options for differentiating sources, learning processes, and demonstrations of learning.
- As or after you generate a list of possibilities, engage in discussions with a small group or a partner about which strategies might work best for your students in the unit you are planning. You can engage in parallel planning (side-by-side planning on different lessons) or collaborative planning (planning with a colleague who is working on the same lesson or unit).

Professional Practice
- Identify high-impact strategies from the possibilities generated in the collegial exploration and discussion.
- Use at least three of the strategies in your instructional program and come to the next session prepared to share how it went, what you learned, the impact on student learning, and next steps.

Scaffolding Sort

Purposes
- Identify multiple categories of readiness
- Identify an array of scaffolding possibilities
- Evaluate and select scaffolding options based on categories of readiness or for individual students

Time
45 minutes

Materials
- *Instruction for All Students* pages 201-203
- A copy of **Tool VIII-4: Scaffolding Sort** for each participant

Process
- Read page 201 in *Instruction for All Students*: **What is Scaffolding?**
- Discuss how scaffolding instruction is like the scaffolding used in building construction.
- Scan the scaffolding options on pages 202-203: **Fifty Ways to Scaffold Learning**.
- Distribute **Tool VIII-4: Scaffolding Sort**.
- Select one of the following systems to sort the scaffolding options.
  - Identify up to six students who would benefit from more scaffolding of instruction. Place the name of one student at the top of each of the boxes. Sort through the strategies and list the strategies that might be helpful for each of the students listed. OR
  - Sort the scaffolding strategies into the following categories of student need: **Reading, Writing, Organization, Attention, Language Acquisition, and Persistence/Task Completion**. Write a category at the top of each box on the **Scaffolding Sort** handout.

Professional Practice
Use the selected scaffolding strategies in your classroom practice and be prepared to share in the next session what impact these strategies had on student learning.

Key Ideas to Review/Connections to Make
- **Task Analysis**: pages 46-47
- **Struggling Learners**: page 199
- **Unsuccessful Readers and Helping Unsuccessful Readers Be Successful**: pages 79-80

Repertoire Building Jigsaw
Readiness, Interests, and Information Processing Styles

Purposes
- Validate current practice and to build repertoire in planning for student diversity in readiness, interests, and information processing styles
- Provide an opportunity to implement new and/or refined approaches to meeting the needs of diverse learners
- Receive encouragement and feedback from colleagues while integrating new strategies into instructional practice

Time
- 30 minutes for session
- 30 to 60 additional minutes depending on extensions selected

Materials
- *Instruction for All Students* pages 211-216
- See optional **Extending the Learning** exercises on the following page for additional pages in *Instruction for All Students* and one handout

Process
- Jigsaw the reading of pages 211-216 in *Instruction for All Students*.
  - **Modalities and Learning Preferences**: pages 204-205
  - **Interest Grouping**: pages 211-212
  - **Anchoring Activities**: pages 213-214
  - **Tiered Assignment Example**: pages 215-216
- After reading the assigned pages, share your insights by discussing validations for current practice and implications for future practice you found on those pages.

Professional Practice
Select at least one of the chunks of information studied and apply it in your instructional program. Come to the next session ready to explain what you tried, why you selected that approach, what you learned, and next steps with this learning.

Repertoire Building Jigsaw

Extending the Learning with a Focus on Multiple Intelligences
- This extension could be done as **Professional Practice** with a follow-up **Collegial Conversation** or in a 30-minute session.
- Prepare and distribute copies of **Active Learning Strategies through the Lens of Multiple Intelligences (VIII-5)**.
- Review the key ideas, strategies, and examples related to multiple intelligences theory on pages 50 and 127-132 in *Instruction for All Students*.
- Review **Chapter IV: Active Learning** following the directions listed on the handout.
- Engage in discussions with a small group or partner about how your can ensure that all students are given opportunities to use their learning preferences and strengths through the purposeful use of the active learning strategies.
- Note availability of **Tool II-11: Multiple Intelligences Unit Map**.

Extending the Learning with a Focus on Student Choice
- This extension could be done as **Professional Practice** with a 15 minute follow-up **Collegial Conversation** or in a 30 minute session.
- Read page 258: **Top 10 Questions for Secondary Teachers** in *Instruction for All Students*. While this page is addressed to secondary teachers the questions are equally applicable to elementary classrooms.
- Jot down your responses to each of the questions and to be prepared to engage in discussion about your responses.
- Use the Carolyn Mamchur quote at the bottom of page 258 to structure the collegial discussion.

Self-Assessment
Inclusive Instruction

How is teaching advanced and struggling learners like and different? In reality, the same principles should apply to both. Compare and contrast your instructional approach with these learners.

Teaching Advanced Learners

How do you...

1. Discover and acknowledge what they already know.

2. Provide a balance of skill building and meaning making activities.

3. Plan and guide them in planning projects that capitalize on their interests.

4. Allow them some flexibility in the way they use their time.

5. Allow them to learn at a different pace than their peers.

6. Plan a variety of relevant learning experiences; both teacher and students monitor the effectiveness.

7. Help them to be aware of and use productive learning strategies.

8. Teach them to be self-sufficient; only do for them as much as you need to do.

9. Encourage them to demonstrate mastery in a wide variety of ways.

Teaching Struggling Learners

How do you...

1. Discover and acknowledge what they already know.

2. Provide a balance of skill building and meaning making activities.

3. Plan and guide them in planning projects that capitalize on their interests.

4. Allow them some flexibility in the way they use their time.

5. Allow them to learn at a different pace than their peers.

6. Plan a variety of relevant learning experiences; both teacher and students monitor the effectiveness.

7. Help them to be aware of and use productive learning strategies.

8. Teach them to be self-sufficient; only do for them as much as you need to do.

9. Encourage them to demonstrate mastery in a wide variety of ways.

Getting Started with Differentiation

Differentiation of instruction does not mean that you individualize instruction or provide something "different" from the normal lesson for a few struggling or advanced students. It means that you think proactively and, from the beginning, the "normal" lesson includes more than one avenue for success. It means that you think about the diversity of your learners when you are planning and don't ever again fall into the trap of thinking that "one size fits all." Use what you already know about the SBE Planning Process and meeting the needs of diverse learners to answer the following questions.

1. Identify a standard/benchmark/indicator you will be addressing in the near future.

2. What assessment opportunities might you give students to demonstrate what they have learned about the above concept?

3. Given the task analysis, what information and skills should all students experience? List a few instructional strategies and practice and/or processing activities which would facilitate that learning.

Getting Started with Differentiation

Multiple pathways thinking begins here!

4. What might you do to extend and expand the thinking of students ready to and/or interested in going beyond what you've planned? Include both inside and outside of class possibilities.

5. What do you know about your struggling learners that you need to address up front? What about your ESL students? Your special education students? List specific examples of instruction strategies, adaptations, and support systems that would be helpful to small groups?

6. What might you do to re-teach or help students having difficulties in understanding this concept? Include both inside and outside of class possibilities.

Differentiating Sources, Learning Processes, and Demonstrations of Learning for the study of _____

Sources of Information	Learning Processes Including Assignments and Homework	Ways Students Can Show What they Know
See pages 14-19, 62-82, 88-89, 133, 240-247, 229-230.	See pages 14, 16-19, 85-120, 124-148, 204-204, 225-239.	See pages 127-140, 151-174, 180, 183-184, 206-210, 231-232, 235.

© Just ASK Publications

Active Learning Strategies through the Lens of Multiple Intelligences Theory

Review the **Active Learning Stategies** listed below through the lens of **Multiple Intelligences Theory**. On the line next to the strategy name, write the name(s) of the intelligence preference it addresses.

_____ **Corners** (Kagan)
_____ **Frame of Reference**
_____ **Graffiti**
_____ **Inside-Outside Circles** (Kagan)
_____ **Sort Cards**
_____ **I Have the Question, Who Has the Answer?**
_____ **All Hands on Deck**
_____ **Five Card Draw**
_____ **Tic-Tac-Toe**
_____ **Learning Buddies**
_____ **Line-Ups** (Kagan)
_____ **Numbered Heads Together** (Kagan)
_____ **Scavenger Hunt**
_____ **Stir the Class**
_____ **Take A Stand**
_____ **Exclusion Brainstorming**
_____ **Facts & Folklore**
_____ **Anticipation/Reaction Guide**
_____ **Personal Opinion Guide**
_____ **Think-Pair-Share**
_____ **Three-Column Chart**
_____ **3-2-1**
_____ **Ticket to Leave**
_____ **Walking Tour**
_____ **Connection Collection**
_____ **ABC to XYZ**

Thinking Skills
for the 21st Century

IX

Self-Assessment

Collegial Conversations

Build in time at the beginning of each session for collegial discussions about how you used previous learning in your classrooms and professional practice. See page 275 in *Instruction for All Students* for questions to frame these discussions.

Self-Assessment

Purposes
- Surface key variables to consider when designing rigorous learning experiences
- Provide data to frame discussions about decision-making in lesson and unit design

Time
20 minutes

Materials
- *Instruction for All Students* pages 9, 12-13 and 219-248
- **Self-Assessment: 21st Century Thinking Skills** page 219 in *Instruction for All Students* or a copy of **Tool IX-1: Self-Assessment: 21st Century Thinking Skills** for each participant

Process
- Read **Results That Matter** section on pages 9, 12-13, and 248 in *Instruction for All Students* for background information on 21st century thinking skills.
- Complete the **Self-Assessment: 21st Century Thinking Skills**. Use page 219 or distribute copies of **Tool IX-1: Self-Assessment: 21st Century Thinking Skills**.
- Discuss with a neighbor or in table groups what you discovered about how your instructional practice is or is not aligned with the thinking skills needed for the 21st century.

21st Century Thinking Skills in Action

Purpose
- Consider eight categories of 21st century thinking skills
- Analyze practitioner examples, descriptions of structures, taxonomies, and models of teaching for the categories of 21st century thinking skills

Time
45 minutes

Materials
- ***Instruction for All Students*** pages 220-230 and 239-247
- A copy of **Tool IX-2: 21st Century Thinking Skills Circles** for each participant

Process
- Turn to pages 220-221 in ***Instruction for All Students*** and take a tour through the categories of 21st century thinking skills found in the circles.
- Discuss what you see there and add any other thinking skills you think should be included.
- Distribute **Tool IX-2: 21st Century Thinking Skills Circles**.
- Work collaboratively to identify the kinds of thinking each of the examples and lesson descriptions on pages 222-230 requires. Many will fit in more than one category of thinking skills.

Professional Practice
- Monitor the assignments you make and the questions you ask between now and the next session.
- Make note of the categories of thinking skills listed on pages 220 and 221 that you use automatically and those that you have to make a conscious effort to include.
- Come to the next session with a goal statement written as to your next steps in refining your practice around including 21st century thinking skills in your instructional design. Title your goal statement: **Ways I Can Promote 21st Century Thinking Skills**.
- Be ready to share your goal statement and a draft action plan with colleagues.

Using Bloom's Taxonomy

Purposes
- Revisit Bloom's Taxonomy in its original form and consider it in two new formats
- Practice designing tasks and questions that are aligned with the indicators embedded in the learning standards and curriculum documents of your district

Time
60 minutes

Materials
- *Instruction for All Students* pages 231-235
- A copy of **Tool IX-3: Using Bloom's Taxonomy** for each participant

Process
- Read pages 231-235 in *Instruction for All Students* and complete the exercise on page 233.
- Distribute **Tool IX-3: Using Bloom's Taxonomy** and follow the directions on that document. Be purposeful about crafting assignments and questions that are at or above the level of understanding required by the indicator or benchmark you select. You may start at a lower level but you need to continue the design of tasks and questions until practices and rehearsals for the level or understanding required by the standards are included in the design.

Professional Practice
- Use the tasks and questions designed in the **Bloom's Taxonomy** exercise.
- Come to the next session ready to share the implementation successes and struggles.

Extending the Learning with Williams' Taxonomy
- This exercise could be done as **Professional Practice** with a 15 minute follow-up **Collegial Conversations** session or in a 30 minute session.
- Use *Instruction for All Students* pages 236-238.
- Read page 237 and collaboratively complete the exercise on page 238.
- Identify a concept you will be teaching in the near future and use the **Teacher's Guide to Williams' Taxonomy** on page 236 to develop a series of learning experiences around that concept.
- Note that this guide is available as **Tool IX-4: Williams' Taxonomy**.

Self-Assessment
21st Century Thinking Skills

Consider whether or not these statements represent your own professional practice.
A (Almost Always), S (Sometimes), N (Not Yet)

_____ I ask students to go beyond the factual level and think at the conceptual level.

_____ I pose questions and create learning experiences that cause students to challenge their current thinking and consider alternatives.

_____ I ensure that when technology is used as a learning tool, the learning experiences are designed to include the use of a wide array of thinking skills as students access, respond to, communicate, and create information and ideas.

_____ I design learning experiences in which thinking processes are named, modeled, and practiced in a variety of situations.

_____ I ask students to reflect on and monitor the effectiveness of their thinking.

_____ I structure the learning environment so that all skill building and information input leads to opportunities to make personal meaning and connections to life beyond the classroom.

_____ I provide opportunities for students to respond to and ask thought-provoking questions.

_____ I consider the levels of Bloom's Taxonomy when planning instruction and build on Bloom's in ways that promote rigor and relevance.

_____ I build decision making and problem solving situations into learning experiences.

_____ I setup situations where students use collaborative thinking and communication skills and then analyze and reflect on the effectiveness of actions.

Thinking Skills for the 21ˢᵗ Century

Creative Thinking

?

Metacognitive Thinking
(thinking about your thinking)

Conceptual Thinking
(includes creative, critical, and Metacognative thinking)

Aha!

Introspective Thinking

!

© Just ASK Publications   Tool IX-2   *Instruction for All Students Facilitator's Handbook*

Thinking Skills for the 21ˢᵗ Century

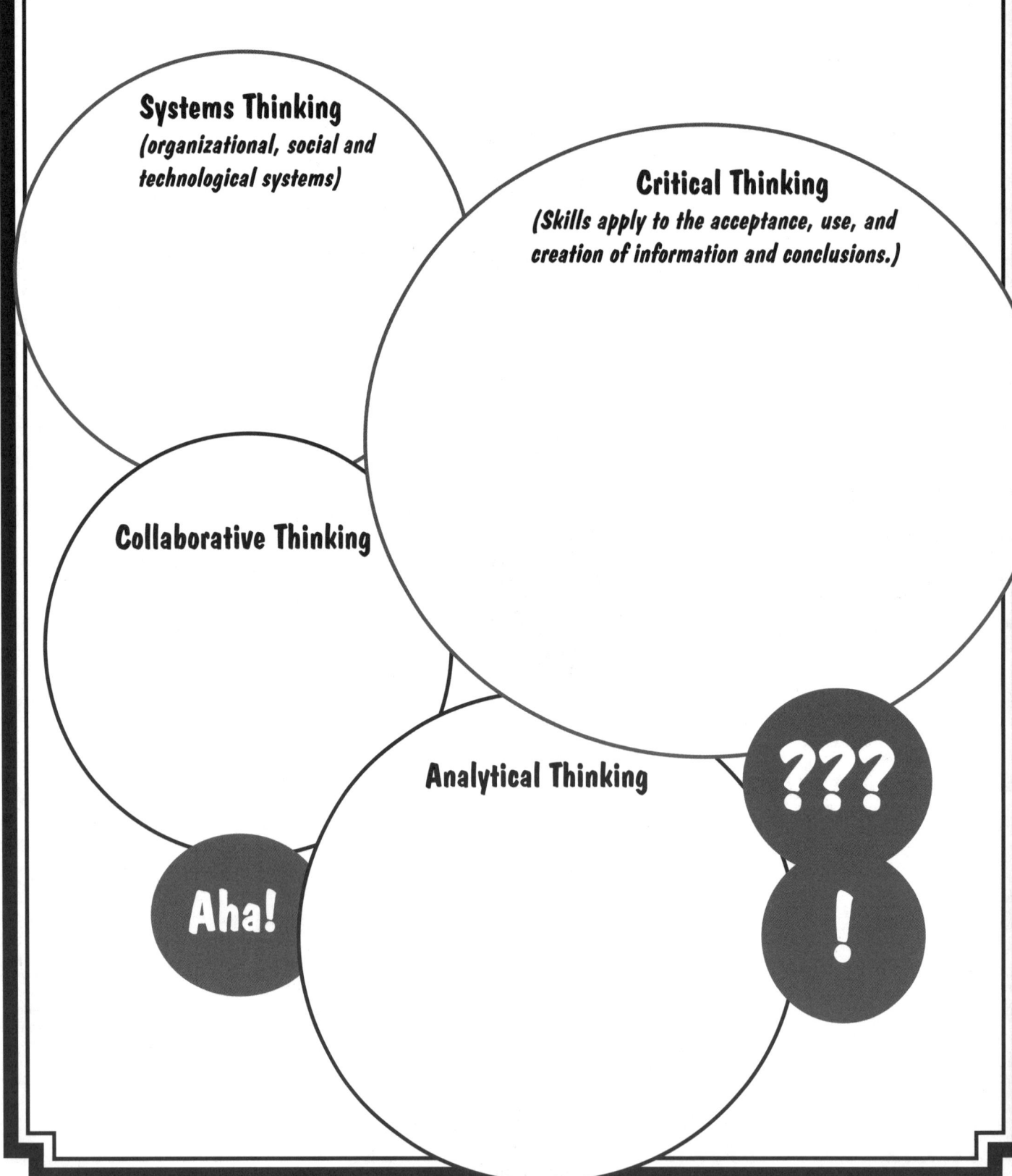

Using Bloom's Taxonomy

Identify standard, benchmark, indicator, or key concepts to be studied. _____
_____

Use this form to:
- Design questions, Learning experiences, and assessments for the entire class.
- Design different questions or learning experiences for small groups of students.
- Design questions and learning experiences and have students choose which to complete.

Consult pages 231-235 in *Instruction for All Students* for suggestions.

Knowledge
Students recall facts and information

- Match

- List

- Sequence

Comprehension
Students explain in their own words and summarize information

- Interpret

- Restate/paraphrase

- Draw/illustrate

- Give examples

Application
Student use information in new situations/ways
- Classify

- Transfer

- Apply in a real world or interdisciplinary situation

-

-

-

Analysis
Students examine component parts
- How is _____ like and different from _____?

- Graph data and prepare report

- Categorize

- Cause and effect

-

-

-

Synthesis
Students put components/elements together differently to create a new solution, product, or approach.

- Create

- Write a new _____ from the perspective of _____

- Restructure/reorganize

- Imagine

-

-

Evaluation
Students develop and articulate opinions supported by evidence and logical reasoning

- Judge

- Decide if ... and provide data to support your decision

- Appraise the value

- Write a recommendation

-

-

Williams' Taxonomy

Fluency

Name as many _____ as you can in 60 seconds.

Flexibility

Classify the _____ listed in the fluency exercise. Use a unique classification system.

Originality

Think of a unique way to...

Elaboration

Explain what you think it would be like today if...

Risk-Taking

If you compared yourself to a _____, what kind of _____ would you resemble?

Curiosity

If you could meet a/an _____, what would you want to know about...?

Complexity

Describe or design an object or machine that you could make from _____.

Imagination

Imagine that _____ could talk. What would they say to/about...?

The Learning Environment

X

Communicating High Expectations

Collegial Conversations
Build in time at the beginning of each session for collegial discussions about how you used previous learning in your classrooms and professional practice. See page 275 in **Instruction for All Students** for questions to frame these discussions.

Self-Assessment: Communicating High Expectations

Purpose
- Examine current practices for their potential to promote students' sense of self-efficacy
- Identify areas of focus for increasing frequency and quality of high expectations messages

Time
15 minutes

Materials
Instruction for All Students page 251 or a copy of **Tool X-1: Self-Assessment: Ways to Communicate High Expectations** for each participant

Process
- After **Collegial Conversations** turn to page 251 or distribute copies of **Tool X-1: Self-Assessment: Ways to Communicate High Expectations**.
- Complete the self-assessment and then engage in a discussion with a small group or a partner about what you discovered as you completed the self-assessment. Additionally, discuss how what you read in other chapters on 21st century thinking skills, active learning, differentiation, feedback, etc, communicates high expectations for learning.

Building Student Responsibility

Purposes
- Build skills at helping students self-assess and self adjust
- Expand repertoire of strategies that deal with unmet expectations, focus on the future, and have the potential to increase learning

Time
45-60 minutes

Materials
- *Instruction for All Students* pages 252-261
- A table set for each table or a copy of the following tools for each participant
  - **Tool X-2: Incomplete Assignment Log**
  - **Tool X-3: Contract for Improvement Points**
  - **Tool X-4: Error Analysis**
  - **Tool X-5: Daily Log**
  - **Tool X-6: Skill Building and Meaning Making**
  - **Tool X-7: Learning Log**
  - **Tool X-8: Reflections on the Week**
- A copy of **Tool X-9: 3-2-1** for each participant

Process
- Read pages 252-254 in *Instruction for All Students* and discuss how the **Error Analysis** chart on page 254 promotes student examination of their effort (self-assessment) and to plan future course of actions (self-adjustment). Consider how this error analysis matches a skill set we use in our daily lives.
- Distribute copies of the tools listed in the materials section.
- Examine and discuss how each of the tools would promote a sense of student self-efficacy and responsibility.
- Read pages 259-261. As you read, consider how your current practice is aligned with the recommendations on those pages. Discuss with a small group or a partner what adjustments you could make in your responses to unmet expectations of a given student or group of students so that you can maximize the amount of time and energy you have to focus to high levels of learning.
- Distribute **Tool X-9: 3-2-1**.
- Complete the **3-2-1**; discuss the key points, questions, and actions you listed.

Professional Practice
Take the action you identified on your **3-2-1** and come to the next session ready to discuss what you did and its impact on the learning environment.

Space, Time, and Procedures

Purposes
- Identify practices and procedures that are working well and those that are not working so well
- Seek collegial assistance in building procedural repertoires

Time
60 minutes

Materials
- *Instruction for All Students* pages 262-266
- A copy of **Tool X-10: Procedure Potpourri** for each participant

Process
- Read pages 262-264 in *Instruction for All Students* and discuss the role that room arrangement and time templates play in creating a productive learning environment.
- Read pages 265-266. Use the first paragraph on page 265 to focus a discussion about the effectiveness and efficiency of the procedures currently in place in your classroom.
- Distribute copes of **Tool X-10: Procedure Potpourri**.
- Read through the list and jot down procedures that are working well in your classroom. Add other productive procedures to the end of the list.
- Interact with colleagues in a **Scavenger Hunt** (See pages 104-105) format to seek suggestions from others about possible procedures in the areas you left blank.

Professional Practice
Use one of the **Time Templates** or procedures from the **Procedure Potpourri** exercise in your instructional practice and be prepared to share what worked and what did not work in the **Collegial Conversations** at the next session.

Self-Assessment
Communicating High Expectations

Assess your practice around each of these strategies for letting students know you believe that they are capable of achieving a high level.

Almost Always (A), Sometimes (S), Not Yet (N)

Do you...

_____ 1. **Communicate clear expectations.** Include criteria for success such as rubrics, task performance lists, and exemplars of good performance.

_____ 2. **Model enthusiasm** for what is to be learned, the work to be done, and for student effective efforts and successes.

_____ 3. **Organize the learning environment for thinking.** Carefully plan questions, craft examples, stories, and activities that promote transfer and retention.

_____ 4. **Monitor student attributions and use attribution retraining** with those who make external attributions.

_____ 5. **Provide feedback from multiple sources** so that learners are able to learn from the feedback and make adjustments in their future work.

_____ 6. **Design a brain compatible classroom** through the use of active learning, feedback, and varied sources of input in a safe environment.

_____ 7. **Coach students** in setting challenging yet attainable **goals** and in designing and implementing **action plans** for attaining those goals.

_____ 8. **Include opportunities for all categories of thinking** in discussions with and assignments for low performing students. Teach students to think **about their thinking** and to learn what kind of thinking is required in which situations.

_____ 9. **Promote and teach effective effort strategies such as**
   - task and error analysis
   - choice of sources, processes, and products
   - focus groups for skill development
   - graphing of progress
   - interactive notebooks
   - journal/log entries (cause and effect of effort)

_____ 10. **Scaffold instruction** so that all students have the appropriate levels of support and structure they need to achieve success as learners and withdraw the scaffolding when students are to learn more independently.

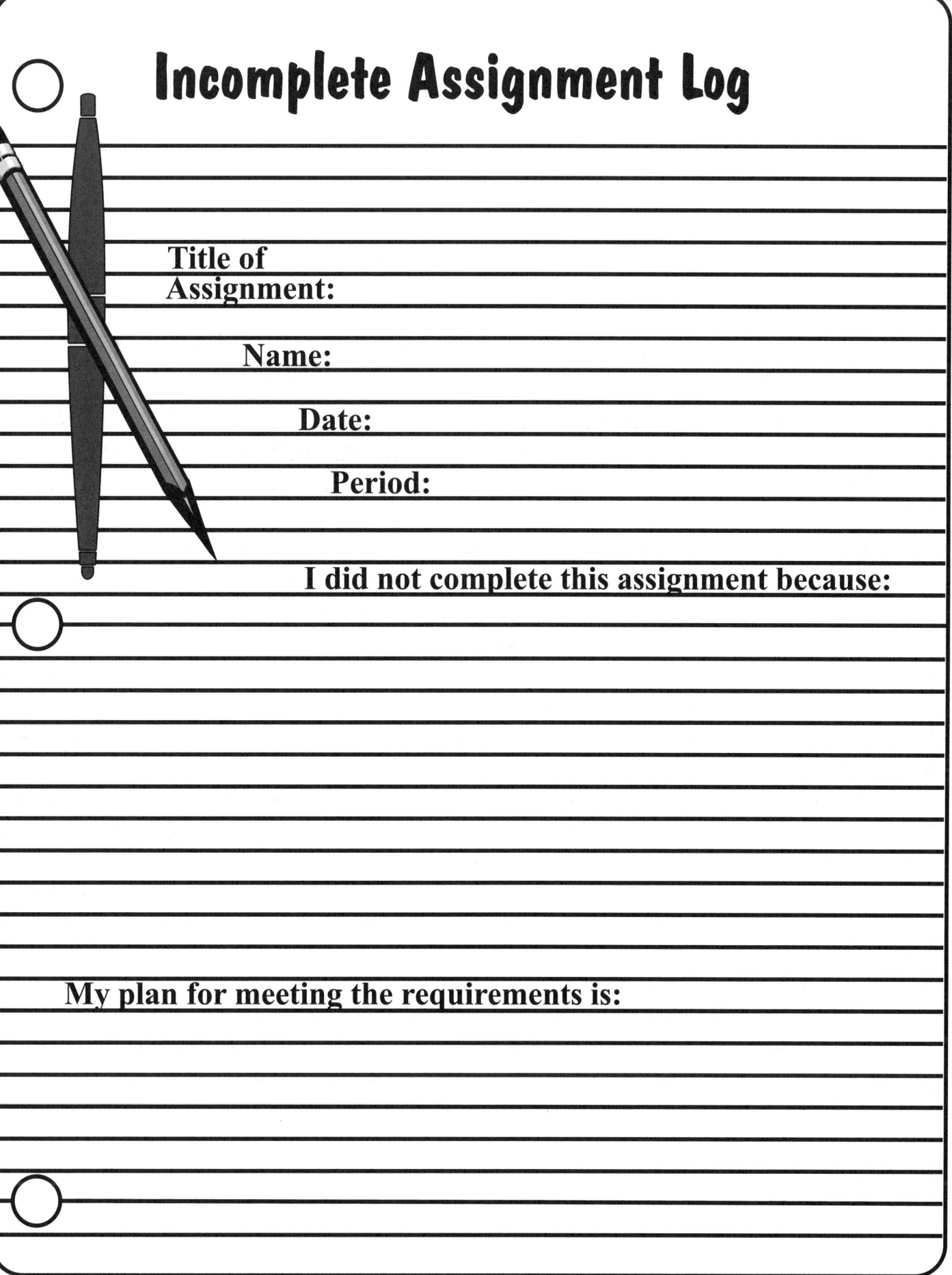

Incomplete Assignment Log

Title of Assignment:

Name:

Date:

Period:

I did not complete this assignment because:

My plan for meeting the requirements is:

© Just ASK Publications Tool X-2 Instruction for All Students Facilitator's Handbook

Contract for Improvement Points

Name:
Class Period: Date:
Title of Work to Be Improved:

I, _____ agree to re-work/re-write the work named above. I will improve the work by addressing the following specifics agreed upon by my teacher and myself. The points I might earn have been assigned and I understand that I must complete the work according to the contract requirements in order to receive full credit.

Specific Improvements   **Points Possible**

1.

2.

3.

4.

5.

6.

Date Improved Work Due: Total:

Signatures:

Error Analysis

Maintain this error analysis chart so that you can become aware of the patterns of errors you are making. This chart is easily adaptable to science, writing, spelling, and the study of foreign languages. Use the variables identified in a task analysis or provided by your teacher.

List types of errors above the columns in the graph.

Date   Assignment/Assessment

Directions:
For each assignment or assessment completed, write the name and date of the assignment or assessment on the lines to the left of the grid. Identify the type of errors made and check the appropriate boxes. At the end of each unit, identify the pattern of errors.

Daily Log for _____
(Date)

Name of Class

Name of Scribe

Standards and Essential

Summary of Activities (include page references and handouts):

Papers Collected:

Work Assigned: **Due Dates:**

Questions Asked/Discussed:

Reminders Given:

Other Important Information:

© Just ASK Publications — Tool X-5 — *Instruction for All Students Facilitator's Handbook*

Journal Entry
Skill Building and Meaning Making

1. What should I know and be able to do at the end of this lesson/unit or experience?

2. What do I already know that will be useful in learning this new material or working in this way?

3. How is this knowledge and how are these skills important in the world outside of school?

4. When are the important check points and deadlines?

5. How will I be able to tell when I have done a really outstanding job?

Learning Log

for the week of _____

MONDAY

Things I Learned
1.
2.

Opinion of My Day

Something on Which I Want to Work Harder and What I Plan To Do

TUESDAY

Things I Learned
1.
2.

Opinion of My Day

Something on Which I Want to Work Harder and What I Plan To Do

WEDNESDAY

Things I Learned
1.
2.

Opinion of My Day

Something on Which I Want to Work Harder and What I Plan To Do

THURSDAY

Things I Learned
1.
2.

Opinion of My Day

Something on Which I Want to Work Harder and What I Plan To Do

Reflections on the Week

Name: _____   Week of: _____

What I Learned This Week:

How I Can Use It:

Areas in Which I Am Making Progress:

I Need to Improve in:

My Goal for Next Week:

What I Enjoyed Most This Week:

3 Ideas I want to discuss
-
-
-

2 Questions I want to ask
-
-

1 Action I want/need to take
-

Procedure Potpourri

Planning procedures and constantly evaluating their effectiveness is crucial in creating a productive learning environment. Read through the regularly occurring events listed below. List possible procedures you might use. After generating a list of possibilities, evaluate each possibility in terms of the time and energy each would cost you. If the record keeping, implementation, or enforcement of any of them would be too time or energy consuming, consider other possibilities. If what you try does not work, try something else. You may want to check with other teachers who teach the same grade or subject. Remember, you are the professional decision maker and only have to consider their suggestions. What works for one person may not work for another.

Entering the classroom

Beginning the school day or the class period

Taking attendance

Students returning from absences

Dealing with tardies

Procedure Potpourri

Distributing materials and student work

Collecting materials and student work

Dealing with broken or missing supplies

Students asking for and receiving help

Making transitions

What to do when work is finished

Restroom visits and requests for drinks

Procedure Potpourri

Gaining student attention

Giving directions

Communicating outcomes and agenda

Structuring small group work

Handling missing or incomplete assignments

Student movement around room

Leaving the classroom/Dismissal

© Just ASK Publications — Tool X-10 — *Instruction for All Students Facilitator's Handbook*

Procedure Potpourri

Procedure for...

Procedure for...

Procedure for...

Procedure for...

Procedure for...

Procedure for...

Procedure for...

Collegial Collaboration

XI

Self-Assessment

Collegial Conversations

Build in time at the beginning of each session for collegial discussions about how you used previous learning in your classrooms and professional practice. See page 275 in *Instruction for All Students* for questions to frame these discussions.

Self-Assessment

Purposes
- Identify collaborative practices that promote professional growth and student learning
- Assess current collaborative practices and plan how to refine and expand such work

Time
30 minutes

Materials
Instruction for All Students pages 10-11
Instruction for All Students page 269 or a copy of **Tool XI-1: Self-Assessment: Collegial Collaboration** for each participant

Process
- Turn to page 269 in *Instruction for All Students* or distribute **Tool XI-1: Self Assessment: Collegial Collaboration**.
- Complete the self-assessment and discuss how your own perceptions of current practice in the team or school match with the perceptions of others.
- Focus on page 268 which provides resources for exploring the implementation of Professional Learning Communities (PLCs).
- **Optional**: Access one of the four websites listed on page 268 and report back at a follow-up meeting about what you learned there.
- Revisit pages 10-11 to review a list of formats for collegial collaboration and to read how one elementary school in Maryland put these constructs in action.
- Engage in partner or small group discussions about how the collaborative work of the staff at Pine Crest Elementary School matches the collaborative practice in your school.

Focus on Data Analysis and Integration

Purposes
- Identify a wide array of data sources
- Promote the use of multiple forms of data to focus discussions and inform decisions

Time
60 minutes

Materials
- *Instruction for All Students* pages 268-291
- A copy of the following tools for each participant
  - **Tool XI-2: Item Indicator Analysis**
  - **Tool XI-3: Cause and Effect Analysis**
- A copy of **Tool XI-4: Data Analysis and Integration** for each participant

Process
- Distribute **Tool XI-4: Data Analysis and Integration**.
- To set the stage for this study, complete this analysis of how your school, team, or department is currently using data to drive discussions and inform practice.
- Then engage in discussion about the relative strengths and weaknesses of each use of data.
- Divide the reading of the following pages and report out about the key ideas and the implications for their practice given the current reality.
  - **Action Research**, **Data Collection Possibilities**, **and Questions to Consider**: pages 271 and 280-282 in *Instruction for All Students*
  - **Looking at Assignments and Student Work**: pages 273 and 283-285
- Upon completion of the reading and discussions, identify one approach you would like to explore in more depth and make plans to work collaboratively with one or more colleagues to do so.

Professional Practice
- Collaboratively implement the identified approach and report back to the larger group at follow-up sessions OR
- If the group is small, identify one approach that the entire group will engage in over time.

Formats for Collegial Conversations

Purposes
- Identify multiple formats for engaging in collegial conversations including book clubs, problem solving, and lesson and curriculum design
- Encourage asking for and providing one another assistance in the planning, implementation, and analysis of teaching and learning

Time
- Reading can be completed as a **Professional Practice** task with follow-up **Collegial Conversation** OR
- 30 minutes for reading and discussion in a session

Materials
Instruction for All Students pages 272-277

Process
- Read the following pages in *Instruction for All Students*
  - **Learning Clubs**: page 272
  - **Focus Groups**: page 274
  - **Collegial Discussions**: page 275
  - **Dynamic Discussions**: pages 276-277
- Engage in discussion about which formats are already embedded in the professional practice of your school, team, or department and which formats have the most potential for use in the near future and why.

Working Together in the Classroom

Purposes
- Explore key concepts around standards-based peer observations
- Examine the fundamentals and options for co-teaching

Time
- Reading can be completed as **Professional Practice** task with 15 minutes follow-up **Collegial Conversation** OR
- 45 minutes for reading and discussion in session

Materials
- *Instruction for All Students* pages 276-279 and 286-289
- A copy of the following tools for each participant
  - **Tool XI-5: Standards-Based Observations I**
  - **Tool XI-6: Standards-Based Observations II**
  - **Tool XI-7: Peer Observations and Learning Walks**
  - **Tool XI-8: Peer Observation Reflections**

Process
- Read pages 276-279 and 285-269 in *Instruction for All Students*.
- Discuss the implications of the readings.
- Distribute the tools listed in the **Materials** section above.
- Discuss how you could use these tools in the recommended low-key approaches to peer observation.

Extending the Learning with Teacher Leaders and Mentors
- If group members are working as teacher leaders or mentors, ask them to read pages 270 and 290-291 in *Instruction for All Students*.
- Ask those functioning in those roles to lead a discussion about how what is written there matches their own experiences as teacher leaders and mentors in your school.
- Have them add additional points that they see as important for all their colleagues to know.

Supplemental, Free Resources at www.justaskpublications.com
Mentoring in the 21st Century e-newsletters:
- February 2007 issue: **Peer Observations Possibilities**
- March 2007 issue: **The Challenges of Collaboration in Inclusive Classrooms**
- April 2007: **What Should We Be Looking for in Classrooms?**

Self-Assessment
Collegial Collaboration
Practices that Promote School Success

Educators who use their knowledge, skills, and energy to engage in the following practices greatly increase the probability of higher student achievement. Given that, assess the way you and your colleagues collaborate. Mark each practice as

Often (O), Sometimes (S), Not Yet (N)

Do we...

_____ analyze standards and design instruction and assessments to match those standards

_____ design and prepare instructional materials together

_____ design and evaluate units together...especially those based on clearly articulated national, state, or local standards

_____ research materials, instructional strategies, content specific methodologies, and curriculum ideas to both experiment with and to share with colleagues

_____ design lesson plans together (both within and across grade levels and disciplines)

_____ discuss/reflect on lesson plans prior to and following the lesson

_____ examine student work together to ensure match to high standards, to refine assignments, and to analyze the results and make adaptations and adjustments for future instruction

_____ observe and be observed by other teachers

_____ analyze practices and their productivity

_____ promote the concepts of repertoire and reflection

_____ teach each other in informal settings and in focus groups

_____ develop, use, and analyze results of common assessments

_____ use meeting time for discussions about teaching and learning rather than administrivia

_____ talk openly and often about what we are learning or would like to learn

_____ concentrate efforts and dialogue on quality and quantity of student learning, rather than on how many chapters have been covered in the text

_____ share with each other what we learn at conferences, in college classes, from professional readings, and other professional development endeavors

Item/Indicator Analysis

Student	Item/Indicator 1	Item/Indicator 2	Item/Indicator 3	Item/Indicator 4	Item/Indicator 5	Item/Indicator 6	Item/Indicator 7	Item/Indicator 8	Item/Indicator 9	Item/Indicator 10
Class Average										

Cause/Effect Analysis

Desired Effect - What were the **desired** group and/or individual assessment results?

Effect - What were the **actual** group and/or individual assessment results?

Cause: Methods

Methods used this time:	Potential changes for next time:

Cause: Materials

Materials used this time:	Potential changes for next time:

Cause: People

People involved this time:	Potential changes for next time:

Cause: Time

Time used this time:	Potential changes for next time:

© Just ASK Publications — Tool XI-3 — *Instruction for All Students Facilitator's Handbook*

Data Analysis and Integration

We use data to:	Skillful Use	Learning to Use	Need to Learn
• build a body of evidence to include classroom, district, state, and national data			
• improve the instructional program			
• provide teachers feedback on the effects of their efforts			
• provide students feedback on their performance			
• develop a common understanding of what quality student performance is and how close we are to achieving it			
• measure program results, efficiency, and cost effectiveness			
• understand if what we are doing is making a difference over time by tracking students			
• understand if what we are doing is making a difference over time by examining programs, curriculums, and departments			
• ensure that students/groups of students "do not fall through the cracks" by disaggregating the data in multiple ways			
• identify cause and effect relationships			
• guide curriculum development, integration, and revision			
• develop School Improvement Plans			
• design professional development plans			
• meet district, state, and federal requirements			

Areas of Focus for
Standards-Based Observations I

Use this form to plan observations. Select no more than two or three areas of focus.

_____ How are standards, or what a student must know and be able to do, communicated to students? How is the learning "framed" so that students know what to do and why?

_____ How does the teacher diagnostically determine what students already know related to a standard?

_____ How is students' prior knowledge used to facilitate new learning?

_____ How are new concepts or skills introduced?

_____ What strategies are used to support students in "making meaning" of information and concepts?

_____ How are questions, activities, and assignments all shown to be linked to support students in achieving content standards?

_____ How are multiple ways to learn provided to students with different skills, knowledge levels, abilities, and interests?

_____ How is student learning monitored as the lesson progresses?

_____ How does the teacher seek to clarify information, or clear up misunderstandings or misinformation that is detected?

_____ How is feedback on student work or learning provided?

_____ How is the lesson adjusted in progress as the teacher becomes aware of student responses to instruction?

_____ How is student learning formally assessed?

_____ How do students assess their own and others' work?

Areas of Focus for
Standards-Based Observations II

Use this form to plan peer coaching or peer poaching observations. You can also use it with videotaped classroom episodes. Select two or three areas of focus.

_____ Match of lesson to standards
Specifically:

_____ Classroom routines and procedures
Specifically:

_____ Classroom arrangement of space, furniture, learning materials
Specifically:

_____ Management of student learning groups
Specifically:

_____ Dealing with student behavior issues
Specifically:

_____ Giving instructions for student work
Specifically:

_____ Questioning strategies
Specifically:

_____ Strategies for providing feedback on student work
Specifically:

_____ Strategies for working with special needs students in the regular classroom
Specifically:

_____ Transitions between instructional activities
Specifically:

_____ Literacy/numeracy strategies in the content area
Specifically:

_____ Uses of instructional technology
Specifically:

Data Log for
Peer Observations and Learning Walks

Teacher's Name _____

Date _____

Subject/Grade _____

Focus of Observation/Learning Walk (Optional) _____

Standards/Indicators being addressed:

Students were:

Teacher was:

Evidence of rigor:

Evidence of positive and productive environment:

Points to Ponder:

Peer Observation Reflections

Teacher Observed _____ **Subject** _____

Date _____ **Grade** _____

This sheet reflects my thoughts about:

- ☐ Planning
- ☐ Rigor
- ☐ Literacy
- ☐ Presentation Modes
- ☐ Framing the Learning
- ☐ Real World Connections
- ☐ Active Student Learning
- ☐ Formative Assessment
- ☐ Collaborative Learning
- ☐ Differentiation of Instruction

Organizational Systems for:
- ☐ Instructional Materials
- ☐ The Classroom
- ☐ Students
- ☐ Student Learning

Ahas!	Questions that surfaced

Resources I liked	Ideas to use in my classroom

© Just ASK Publications — Tool XI-8 — *Instruction for All Students Facilitator's Handbook*

Appendix

Resources to Support Learning Communities

Instruction for All Students CD-ROM Table of Contents

This document is the table of contents for the CD-ROM at the back of the book ***Instruction for All Students***. Some of these tools are incorporated into the ***Facilitator's Handbook*** but some are not. Please note that the numbering system for these tools is different and the tool numbers may not necessarily match with those listed in the ***Facilitator's Handbook***.

Standards-Based Unit Exemplars

The following units are used with **Learning Experience II-4: Unit Design in the Standards-Based Classroom**:
- Second Grade - Ghana
- Middle School Science - Force and Motion

E-Newsletters

Access the archives of Just ASK's free e-newsletters at www.justaskpublications.com.
- ***Just for the ASKing!*** - Issue categories that support learning communities include Best Practice in Instruction, Assessment, and Meeting the Needs of Diverse Learners.
- ***Mentoring in the 21st Century*** - This e-newsletter includes timely instructional tips mentors can share with new teachers.

Instruction for All Students
CD-ROM Table of Contents

Chapter II Lesson and Unit Design
II - 1 Self-Assessment - Course and Unit Planning
II - 2 Standards-Based Education - What Elements Are You Using
II - 3 Standards-Based Planning Process
II - 4 A Guide to Unit Design in the Standards-Based Classroom
II - 5 The Top Ten Questions
II - 6 Task Analysis T-Chart
II - 7 Unit Plan A
II - 8 Unit Plan B
II - 9 Unit Plan C
II - 10 Unit Organizer Map
II - 11 Multiple Intelligences Unit Map
II - 12 Unit Design Brainstorming Map
II - 13 Lesson Planning Guide
II - 14 Course Map
II - 15 Standards-Based Instruction Planning Matrix

Chapter III Presentation Modes
III - 1 Self-Assessment - Framing the Learning

Chapter IV Active Learning
IV - 1 Self-Assessment - Active Learning
IV - 2 Frame of Reference
IV - 3 Clock Buddies
IV - 4 Color Wheel Buddies
IV - 5 Canadian Collaborators
IV - 6 Elements Buddies
IV - 7 Parent Function Partners
IV - 8 Book Buddies
IV - 9 South America Learning Buddies
IV - 10 Los Compañeros de Clase
IV - 11 Scavenger Hunt - Find Someone Who
IV - 12 Stir the Class
IV - 13 Three-Column Chart
IV - 14 3-2-1
IV - 15 Active Learning Log

Chapter V Assignments
V - 1 Self-Assessment - Assignments
V - 2 RAFT
V - 3 Homework Planning Guide

Chapter VI The Assessment Continuum
VI - 1 Self-Assessment - Classroom Assessment
VI - 2 Assessing My Assessment
VI - 3 Assessment Planning Guide
VI - 4 Rubric Design Guide
VI - 5 Individual Participation Guide
VI - 6 Peer and Self-Assessment

Chapter VIII Differentiation of Instruction
VIII - 1 Self-Assessment - Inclusive Instruction
VIII - 2 How I'll Show What I Know
VIII - 3 Getting Started with Differentiation
VIII - 4 Tiered Assignments

Chapter IX Thinking Skills for the 21st Century
IX - 1 Self-Assessment - 21st Century Thinking Skills
IX - 2 Skill Building and Meaning Making
IX - 3 Learning Log
IX - 4 Reflections on the Week
IX - 5 Williams' Taxonomy
IX - 6 Decisions-Decisions

Chapter X The Learning Environment
X - 1 Self-Assessment - Ways to Communicate High Expectations
X - 2 Incomplete Assignment Log
X - 3 Contract for Improvement Points
X - 4 Error Analysis
X - 5 Daily Log
X - 6 Procedure Potpourri

Chapter XI Collegial Collaboration
XI - 1 Self-Assessment - Collegial Collaboration
XI - 2 Data Analysis
XI - 3 Item Indicator Analysis
XI - 4 Cause and Effect Analysis
XI - 5 Standards-Based Observations I
XI - 6 Standards-Based Observations II
XI - 7 Peer Observations and Learning Walks
XI - 8 Peer Observation Reflections

Standards-Based Unit Exemplars
Second Grade - Ghana
Middle School Science - Force and Motion

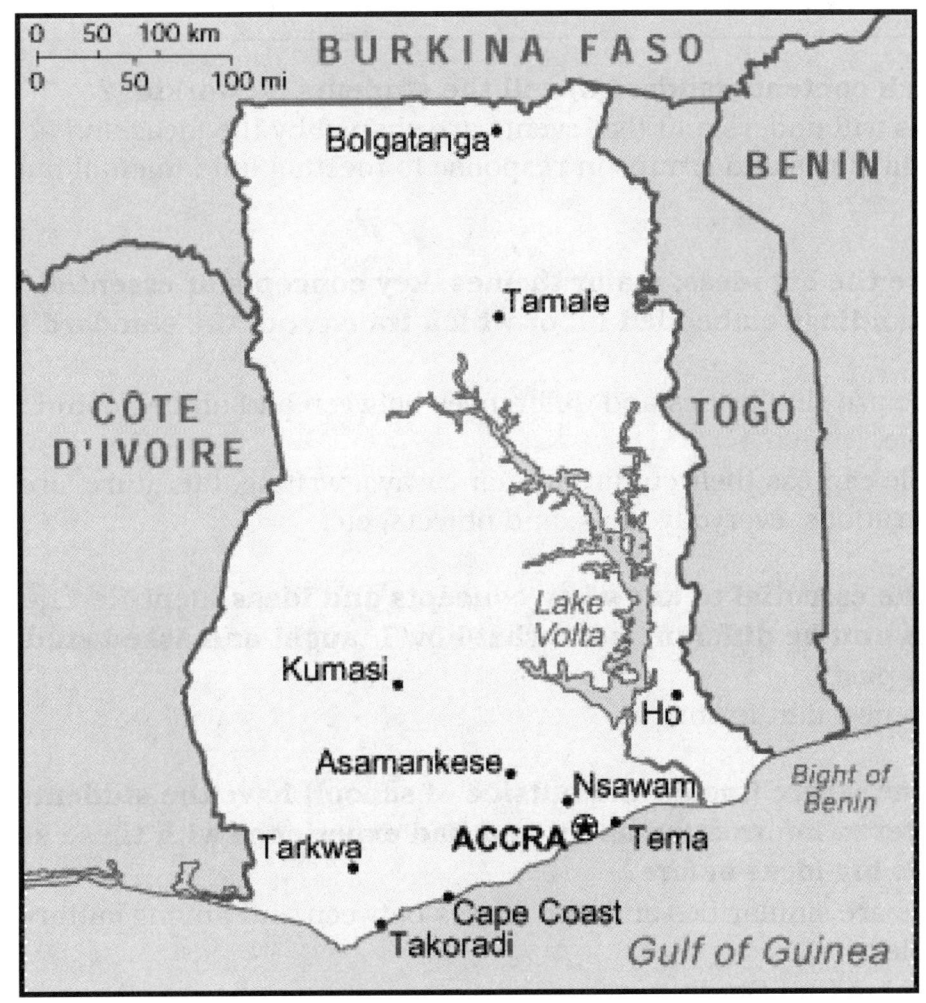

Laura Cork
Bowen Elementary School
Newton Public Schools, Massachusetts

Second Grade
Social Studies Unit: Ghana

1st Oval BEGINNING WITH THE END IN MIND: What should students know and be able to do?

1. **On which content standard(s) will the students be working?**
   Students will understand that events are shaped by the ideas and actions of both individuals and groups in response to meeting fundamental human needs.

2. **What are the big ideas, major themes, key concepts or essential understandings embedded in, or which transcend, the standard listed above?**
   - There are similarities and differences between and among cultures of people.
   - People express their culture in many ways: writing, literature, architecture, celebrations, everyday tools, and objects, etc.

3. **Given the essential to know/key concepts and ideas identified in #2, how will this unit be different from what/how I taught and asked students to do in years past?**
   This is a new unit for me

4. **When and where (inside and outside of school) have the students encountered information about and had experience with these key concepts/big ideas before?**
   - There are similarities and differences between and among cultures of people
     - China Unit Study
     - Christian/Jewish/Muslim/Chinese/Japanese/Russian Peers
     - Active Anti-racist curriculum
     - Read Alouds – social justice
   - People express their culture in many ways: writing, literature, architecture, celebrations, everyday tools and objects, etc.
     - China Unit
     - Classmates' backgrounds
     - Read Alouds

2nd Oval ASSESSMENT:
How will my students and I know when they are successful?

5. **What would it look like when students can demonstrate that they understand the big ideas and have the essential skills? That is, what are some ways they might demonstrate their capacity to use the newly learned concepts/information appropriately in a new situation?**

   Students will:
   - Recognize how others' feelings, values, and behaviors vary from one's own.
   - Identify ways in which people of Ghana satisfy basic human needs.
   - Describe cultural expressions of Ghana's people.
   - Compare and contrast expressions of their own culture with Ghanaian culture.
   - Compare and contrast the lives of people from Ghana, China, Mexico and the U.S.

6. **What tasks/products would demonstrate student understanding? Should I use a rubric or a performance task list and what criteria should be included?**
   - **Postcards from Ghana**
     - Choose a city/village in Ghana to write home about as if you are visiting that place right now.
     - Write a postcard to your family telling about your stay in this place, detailing what you see, hear, and smell.
     - Use at least one sentence to explain how you are surprised about discovering how the people in this place live similarly to you. Use at least one sentence to describe how the people in their place are different from you. (Other than looks!)
     - Use complete sentences, appropriate punctuation and correct spelling.
     - Illustrate the front of the post card to show the place you choose using crayons, colored pencils, or collage. The details of your illustration and the written portion of the postcard must match!

   - **RAFT**: You, a travel writer, are preparing a review on your recent trip to Ghana for the next issue of National Geographic for Kids. Fill and bring a suitcase to school as if you just returned from Ghana. Include objects and symbols that represent the ways culture is expressed in Ghana through literature, architecture, food, celebrations, education, and everyday tools. Write 2-3 complete sentences for each object in your suitcase describing the item, its importance in the Ghana culture, and how it is used. Be prepared

to discuss the contents of your suitcase with a small group of listeners interested in visiting Ghana. (Appendix A shows the Analytic Rubric.)
An exemplary suitcase will include:
- A map/globe highlighting Ghana's location in the world and on its continent
- Clothing appropriate for Ghana's climate (i.e. shorts, t-shirts, sandals, hats, rain coats, a school uniform)
- An African game, music or art piece that Ghanaian families may own or use (i.e. Oware, Nte-Too, The Catch, Moonshine Baby, a drum, kente cloth, adinkra)
- A picture of the home you stayed in
- Something she/he bargained for at the market (i.e. utensils, clay pots, baskets, cloth, food, jewelry, fabric, soap, notebooks, pens)
- Something you might take to school with you (i.e. your stool, a pencil, a book/journal for what you learn)
- A short story you have written down that someone in Ghana told you (i.e. an Anansi tale)
- A recipe for a Ghanaian dish or food you would find in Ghana (i.e. oto, fufu balls, potato or rice soup, yams, tomatoes, onions, peppers)

- **Ghana Reflection Sheet**
    - What have you learned about how Ghanaians live? What have you learned about Ghanaian traditions and culture? What have you learned about what is important to Ghanaians?
    - Complete a **Venn Diagram** comparing and contrasting you and a Ghanaian child.

7. **What does a task analysis reveal about the skills, the knowledge and the level of understanding required by the task?**

Skills	Knowledge
Determining importance of materials	Which objects and symbols represent Ghanaian culture
Writing/dictating complete sentences	The importance of the objects/symbols in Ghanaian culture
Giving a talk with appropriate voice	
Level, pacing, eye contact and content	How to prioritize the importance of objects/symbols
	Ghana's writing symbols
	Ghana's climate
	How to write/dictate complete sentences

8. **Do I already have sufficient pre-assessment data or do I need to gather more? What does the pre-assessment data tell me about the skills and knowledge on which the entire group will need to focus? Are there individual students who will need additional support if they are to have a realistic opportunity to demonstrate mastery? In which areas will they need support?**

   - In terms of content, most second graders have extremely limited exposure to Ghanaian culture and therefore start with almost zero background knowledge about its people. However, students do understand, at varying levels, that people live differently depending on where they reside in the world. From their study of China and their own lives, they understand that people speak, eat, practice traditions, and value symbols differently. I will engage students in a **Frame of Reference** activity to gather more specific pre-assessment data that can highlight misconceptions prior to the study.

     In addition, based on my close work with students' writing and speaking performances in other academic areas, I have solid data to plan learning experiences that will enable them to write and speak fluently, clearly, and effectively. Based on my work with students' reading development, I also know which students can easily determine what's most important about a story and what's not, and therefore already have some strength in prioritizing information. I also know which students have difficulty in doing this and will need additional support.

   - J.S. and N.H. will require support for 1) reading text, 2) making realistic comparisons, 3) using time to make connections and comparisons. I will meet with them first and get them to talk about their ideas before having them approach tasks independently. A.T. M.M. N.H. R.J. and T.S. will require support for determining what's most important about what they are learning and then organizing the information for later retrieval. I will coach our literacy aide to help these students practice highlighting "most important details" from their reading and give strong retellings. The whole class will also practice these skills.

3rd Oval LEARNING EXPERIENCES:
What learning experiences will facilitate their success?

9. **How will I "Frame the Learning" so that students know what they are going to be doing, what they will know and be able to do as a result of those activities, how they will be assessed, and how everything they are doing is aligned with the standard?**
   - Explain the "Ghana Must Knows" to start the unit study as what students will know and be able to talk about by the end of the unit. Before each lesson related to this unit, show students which "Must Know" we are working towards understanding.
   - At the beginning of the unit, show students the **Venn Diagram** which they are expected to fill in and discuss.
   - Ask students why they think these are important pieces of knowledge and skills and then discuss with students the importance of 1) visiting parts of the world and being able to appreciate the people and their cultures along the way, 2) being able to work and socialize with people who come from different backgrounds than yourself, and 3) understanding that events are shaped by the ideas and actions of people trying to have their human needs met.
   - Provide students with examples of learning experiences, which they will be engaged in, and show sample products from these experiences that previous students have created to show what they have learned.
   - Explain the travel logs and the RAFT assignment, showing students the performance task list. Highlight the expectations; yet also emphasize the space for choices and creativity.

10. **How will I help students access prior knowledge and use it productively, either building on it or reframing their thinking as appropriate?**
    - Using a **Graffiti**, ask students to think about a child from Ghana coming to visit our country for the first time. In small groups students will visit 6 posters titled: Climate, Families, Transportation, Food, Education and For Fun to record ideas of what that child will learn about America and its culture during a visit.
    - Review similarities and differences between the way we live and how individuals in China live. **Model Thinking Aloud** about and recording predictions for how my life may be similar and different from individuals living in Ghana using a **T-chart**. Pair students to record their own predictions using individual T-charts. Have students share their predictions in small groups. (Identify misconceptions)

- As a whole group, have students generate questions about how Ghanaians may live and what they may value. Post the questions: "What We Wonder/Want to Learn about Ghana."
- Post answers next to the questions as they are discovered throughout the study.

11. **What methods of presentation and what active learning experiences can I use to help students achieve the standard? Could I provide multiple sources of information and exercises that would help all students make real world connections and use sophisticated thinking skills?**
    - **Virtual Tour/Simulation**: Use narrative script to accompany the virtual tour while students pretend/imagine flying to Ghana on British Airways.
    - **Imagery Script** of the four land regions; Teacher reads script while students draw the four regions, imagining themselves in the environment. Then, in small groups, students use a graffiti activity to create word splashes for the four regions. Finally, in partners students create travel brochures to entice tourists to visit a region of choice using the descriptions posted on the corresponding word splash.
    - **Guest Speakers**: Joe and Vida (native Ghanaian) perform a presentation for the class in which they pass around kente cloth, adinkra cloth, demonstrate how to wear the clothing depending on your gender, how to carry goods in a basket on your head, how to carve out a calabash to collect water, how to collect water, how to carry a baby on your back, how students learn by call and repetition in school, how to play the drum, how to perform a native dance, etc.
    - **Video**: Students watch "Georgina Williams of Ghana" then participate in creating a class Venn Diagram and then individually complete their own comparing their own life with the life of Georgina Williams.
    - **Text**: Teacher reads aloud ***Kofi and His Magic*** and organizes literature circles. Prior to the reading, the teacher posts and reviews questions the students will be expected to discuss in small groups following the read aloud. After the read aloud, each student is given a slip of paper with a number on it and one of the posted questions. This paper tells the student his/her group number and the question he/she is responsible for leading and collecting a consensus response to report back to the whole group.
        - In what ways is Kofi a magician?
        - What does Kofe mean when he says "I open my mind?" How and when do you open your mind?
        - What did you learn about the importance of the golden stool?
        - Why do you think the boys' hats with horns made them feel brave? Do you have something you like to wear that makes you feel brave?
        - What information about Kofi's life interested you the most?
        - What more do you want to know about Ghana or Kofi's life?

- Using **Talk, Talk** the teacher (or a guest) demonstrates a storytelling experience based on an Ashanti legend. After the oral retelling of the story, students participate in a **Think-Pair-Share** for several questions requiring students to respond to concepts, elements, and content in the book.
  - What makes the ending clever?
  - How would the story ended differently if the chief's golden stool had spoke before the chief sent the farmer, the fisherman, the weaver, and the bather away?
  - Why was the chief angry when the men told their stories?
  - What parts of this tale could be true? Which parts could be false?
  - Do you think this story is finished? Why?
- **Simulation of meeting a Ghanaian Family**: The grade level teachers bring their classes together and role-play several Ghanaian family members (while showing photographs of these real-life individuals) using a script. After meeting the family, students are asked to think about three questions based on what they just heard, pair with someone else to share their response, and then the partners share their responses with the whole group.
  - *How do many Ghanaian family members help one another?*
  - *How is our Ghanaian family similar to families in the United States?*
  - *How are the Ghanaian family's experiences different from ours?*
- Students analyze a recipe of a typical Ghanaian food they sample. Questions to be asked are: Which ingredients are common to your own diet? Which ingredients are not?
- Through teacher-led discussion, students assess their previous predictions about what they expected to learn about Ghanaian life and culture, and make new predictions.
- In small groups students generate questions collaboratively, with an emphasis on productive questions.
- **Ghana Buddies**: After a lesson, meet with one of your buddies (determined by a Ghanaian city) and summarize one new think you learned, and offer one question you now have.
- Students will log entries into travel journals – what they have seen, experienced, and "What I'm Learning About Ghana."
- **Numbered Heads Together**
  - Name 3 Ghanaian_____ (foods, objects, clothing pieces symbols, etc.)
  - List 3 similarities between your school experience and a Ghanaian child's experience.
  - List 3 differences between your life and either Anusibuno's or Georgina's life.
  - Write 2 ways that Ghanaian life is shaped by where they live in the world.

- Name 2 Ghanaian celebrations.
- List 3 comparisons between your typical food shopping experience and that of a Ghanaians.
- **Sort Cards**
    - In small groups, students generate words and short phrases about Ghana on index cards.
    - Each small group sorts their own cards into self-determined categories.
    - While one person from each group stays at the base table as an expert, the rest of the group tours the classroom to observe whatever categories the groups devised.

12. **What assignments, projects, and homework will help students see the relevance of the learning and help them not only to meet the standard, but retain their learning? How might I provide multiple pathways to learning?**
    - Students learn how to play one Ghanaian game, become an expert in it, and then teach it to others through a jigsaw puzzle activity. After playing students are asked to identify and discuss similarities between the games they became an expert in and a game from their own culture.
    - Students simulate trading at the marketplace using manipulatives to bargain for desired items. Students are then asked to make comparisons between their own grocery experiences and experiences at the marketplace.
    - See Appendix B for homework assignments.
    - Evaluate original and modified predictions – what have we learned?
    - Students share travel journal entries and compare with one another.
    - Small groups discuss what they can expect to learn when visiting other countries.

13. **What classroom activities/observations, as well as formative quizzes and tests would provide my students and me information on their progress toward the standard?**
    - When I listen to students' conversations with their Ghana buddies and read their written comparisons between their own lives and the life of a Ghanaian individual I gain interesting insights into student learning. During these times I frequently check for stereotypes and misconceptions as well as initial understandings of how people are similar and different based on where they live in the world. I also check whether student responses include a balance of information relating to similarities versus differences and how deep the comparisons go. For example, if a student responds to the prompt, "Name one way you and Anusibuno are similar." with "We both eat," I would know the student is not gaining sufficient information to make meaningful comparisons across cultures. However, a student who responds "We both have responsibilities in our families. She has to collect water for the family each morning and I have to set the table at mealtimes"

demonstrates sufficient understanding that people across cultures are similar and different.
- Each student creates and writes a postcard to an American friend (or Japanese, Chinese, or Russian depending on where my students are from) explaining three ways in which his own life is similar to and different from Ghanaian life. Prior to writing, students meet in small groups to generate and record category topics and share them with the whole group. The ease in which each student is able to generate ideas for comparisons informs me of their progress toward the standard.

14. **What materials and resources do I need to locate and organize to provide multiple pathways to learning?**
    - Gather a range of reading level appropriate books
    - Prepare photographs of the concepts to be studied
    - Prepare large maps for classroom display and smaller maps for the students to manipulate
    - Organize games and food recipes (give recipes to room parents for them to prepare)
    - Establish Ghana buddies
    - Bookmark virtual tours
    - Write directions and expectations on chart paper
    - Post "Must Knows" standards
    - Make travel journals and label the "Ghana Crate"
    - Secure exemplars of assignments
    - Teach students how to use a variety of graphic organizers

    How should I organize the classroom and the materials to provide easy student access?
    - Place books on display and in labeled book tubs
    - Keep all the Ghana information together in one part of the classroom
    - Have student work surround the map of Ghana
    - Provide open and closed questions
    - Establish appropriate questions for stand/ sit activities

15. **What else might I do to provide challenging and meaningful experiences for both struggling and advanced learners? Are there other human, prints, or electronic resources I might consult to refine/review my plan?**
    I have strived to embed strategies for reaching both kinds of learners within the previously outlined learning experiences and assessment practices.

4th Oval REFLECTION & DATA ANALYSIS:
Based on data, how do I refine the learning experiences and/or the assessment?

16. **How did students do on the performance task? Were there some students who were not successful? What might account for that? What might I do differently next time?**

17. **What else do I need to consider in my advance planning the next time I am focusing on this standard?**
    I believe that in order for students at this age to make comparisons between their own and another's culture, they need more experience recognizing elements of their own culture (both familial and community). So next time I teach this unit I will spend more time helping students access an understanding of their own culture (and what does and doesn't define culture) before leaping into trying to make comparisons of their own culture. This came clear to me in the Graffiti activity when student responses were limited or stereotypical when asked to write phrases about what a Ghanaian child would learn about American culture if s/he lived with us for a year.

18. **Did all of the activities guide students toward mastery of the standard? Are there activities that need to be added, modified, or eliminated? Am I using these activities because I have always used them or have I analyzed them to be sure that they are the most efficient tools at my disposal?**
    The learning experiences are all very effective in motivating students to learn about a culture quite different from their own and find similarities they can relate to. Students are able to speak of these similarities and differences among themselves, their families, and other adults in the building. During many read-alouds in which other groups of people are represented, students are excitedly noting ways their culture is being expressed and are comparing them to what they learn about Ghanaian culture.

    I would not add additional activities to this unit. However, I would modify several experiences. For example, next time I would:
    - Reduce the amount of writing students are asked to do(i.e. instead of asking students to create their own Venn Diagrams after watching the Georgina Williams video, I would have them write one piece of new information on a post-it note and when we create a class Venn Diagram they add their idea to it.)
    - Provide students with earlier samples and practice with designing a travel brochure.

- Change how students come to understand Ghanaian families instead of having a script read to them with accompanying photographs. I'm not sure how to do this yet, but I am contacting our special guest speakers (natives of Ghana) for more insight.
- Use a chart in the room to collect pertinent vocabulary throughout the study. This collection will help all students access and expand their language in their verbal and written assignments for making more specific comparisons

Each of these changes is based on my analysis of the effective use of the students' time to either gain information or understanding or to demonstrate what they have learned. Each change is based on whether the activity is a meaningful attempt for students to acquire and retain understanding of the standard being taught, or merely serves as a fun "time-filler". Several activities have been modified to reduce the amount of writing students are asked to perform because many of my students were hung up on the process of writing versus having their ideas captured for future reference. In these cases I am comfortable with taking the recording role. I will continue to seek to provide a greater balance of modes for sharing learning through short written phrases, graphic organizers, discussions, pictures, and the creation of material.

19. **Overall, was this unit effective for addressing the standard(s)? Are there other standards that I could incorporate into this unit or are there other units of study where I can have the students revisit these standards or essential understandings?**

    Yes, this unit was very effective for students to explore what constitutes culture and how cultures vary from one another. Learning about other cultures at such an early age is risky. It takes the chance that students won't gain the concepts because they are still figuring out right and left; much less where another country is located, and they are still exploring their own family cultures. However, through this unit, students were able to effectively develop the skills and knowledge needed to draw upon what they already know and integrate it with the ability to make comparisons and begin organizing and communicating new learnings. Prior to this unit, students examined these same standards in a unit on China and will revisit each standard through the next unit of study, Mexico, as applicable to another culture.

GHANA BUDDIES

Name _____

Name _____   Date _____

What's Your Prediction?

One way to make learning easier is to make predictions and then recheck them when you have new information. This afternoon we are going to watch a video about a girl named Georgina from Ghana. In the chart below, make predictions about how your lives may be similar and different.

I predict Georgina and I are similar in that...	I predict Georgina and I are different in that...

Name _____   Date _____

WHAT ARE YOUR INTERESTING IDEAS ABOUT GHANA?

When you hear the word GHANA, what does it make you think of? _____

_____

_____

_____

What is one interesting thing you learned from our "visit" to Ghana? _____

_____

_____

_____

If you could interview Anusibuno, what two questions would you ask her?

1) _____

_____

2) _____

_____

Understanding Ghana: Homework Assignments

Choose one activity to complete for homework each week. Circle each assignment you completed. Bring your weekly product to school each Thursday.

March 8th	March 15th	March 22nd	March 29th	April 5th
Make a map of Ghana that outlines its four main regions. Use different materials/textures to represent each region accurately.	Make up a brief skit showing your morning routine as a Ghanaian child. Your skit should start with you sleeping and end with you arriving at school.	Using some fabric or textured paper design your own small kente cloth.	Imagine going to the market in a village in Ghana. Make a list of what you could trade. Then show what you could realistically expect to trade for your goods.	Write a letter to a friend or relative telling about at least three of the most interesting things you learned about Ghana.
Write a travel review for the Boston Globe About your visit to 1 of Ghana's four regions. Persuade vacationers to visit	Create and Perform your own storytelling of one of your favorite short stories. Use voice changes and include a moral for your story.	Create a song to teach other kids how to count to 10 in a Ghanaian language.	Write a poem describing the atmosphere of a marketplace in Ghana.	Make up at Least four song titles that highlight four things you've learned about Ghana.
Create a painting showing the landscape of one Ghana's four regions. Be prepared to explain why you chose your colors and objects. Your painting will hang in the classroom.	Put together a short scrapbook as if you were a child in Ghana. Include your family, your home, celebrations, traditions, and so on.	Make a list of 10 children's books you would recommend to Anusibuno to learn about how American children live. Explain why you choose 2 of the books.	Tape record a conversation with a vendor at the marketplace when attempting to barter for goods. Have a friend role-play the vendor, but tell him/her what to say *before* you tape record.	Create four different illustrations that represent Ghanaian culture. These illustrations will be used for the backs of a deck of playing cards.

CALLING ALL TRAVELERS!

Show what you know in this GHANA FINAL PROJECT

You, a travel writer, are preparing a review on your recent trip to Ghana for the next issue of National Geographic for Kids. Fill in and bring a suitcase to school as if you just returned from Ghana. Include objects and symbols that represent the ways culture is expressed in Ghana. Think about its geography, home life, schooling, foods, socializing, everyday tools, homes, and so on.

Write 2-3 sentences for each object in your suitcase describing the item, its importance in Ghanaian culture, and how it is used.

Be prepared to discuss the contents of your suitcase with a small group of listeners interested in visiting Ghana.

Use the attached rubric for help.

IN YOUR SUITCASE YOU HAVE BROUGHT BACK:

1) A map/globe showing Ghana's location in the world.
2) Clothing appropriate for Ghana's climate.
3) An African game, music, or art piece.
4) A picture of the home where you stayed.
5) Something you bargained for at the market.
6) Something you would take to school with you
7) A short story you wrote down that someone in Ghana told you
8) A recipe for a Ghanaian dish, or food you would find in Ghana.

GHANA ANALYTIC RUBRIC

Presenter _____ Date _____

Total Score: _____

	16-14 You're ready to write your review!	13-10 You're almost ready to write. Zest it up a little.	9-5 It's hard to write without info and enthusiasm.	4-1 Go back to Ghana! Take notes and photos.
Objects	At least 7 objects/symbols have been appropriately chosen to accurately represent Ghanaian culture **4**	4-6 objects/symbols have been appropriately chosen to accurately represent Ghanaian culture **3**	3 objects/symbols have been chosen to represent Ghanaian culture **2**	1-2 objects/symbols have been chosen to represent Ghanaian culture **1**
Explanations	Each object is accompanied by at least 2-3 complete sentences describing its purpose and value in Ghanaian culture **4**	Each object is accompanied by 2 sentences describing its purpose/value in Ghanaian culture **3**	At least 2 objects are accompanied by complete sentences describing the objects' purpose/value in Ghanaian culture **2**	0 or 1 object is accompanied with a description of its purpose/value in Ghanaian culture **1**
Understanding & Practice	Student shares and discusses the selected objects in a way that demonstrates knowledge, practice and ease **4**	Student shows that s/he mostly understands the content and has practiced his/her presentation **3**	Student shows limited understanding of the content and little practice of his/her presentation **2**	Student shows no understanding or practice of his/her presentation **1**
Creativity & Effort	The project reflects creativity and effort **4**	The project reflects some creativity and effort **3**	The project reflects minimal creativity and effort **2**	The project reflects no creativity or effort **1**

Name _____ Date _____

Ghana Reflection

What was one of the most interesting facts you learned about Ghanaian culture?

_____

_____

_____

_____

What was your favorite learning experience during our study of Ghana?

_____

_____

_____

_____

What about Ghanaian culture do you want to know more about or are left wondering about?

_____

_____

_____

Name _____

Compare how your life is similar to and different from the life of a Ghanaian child. You should have at least three ideas in each section of the Venn Diagram.

Name _____   Date _____

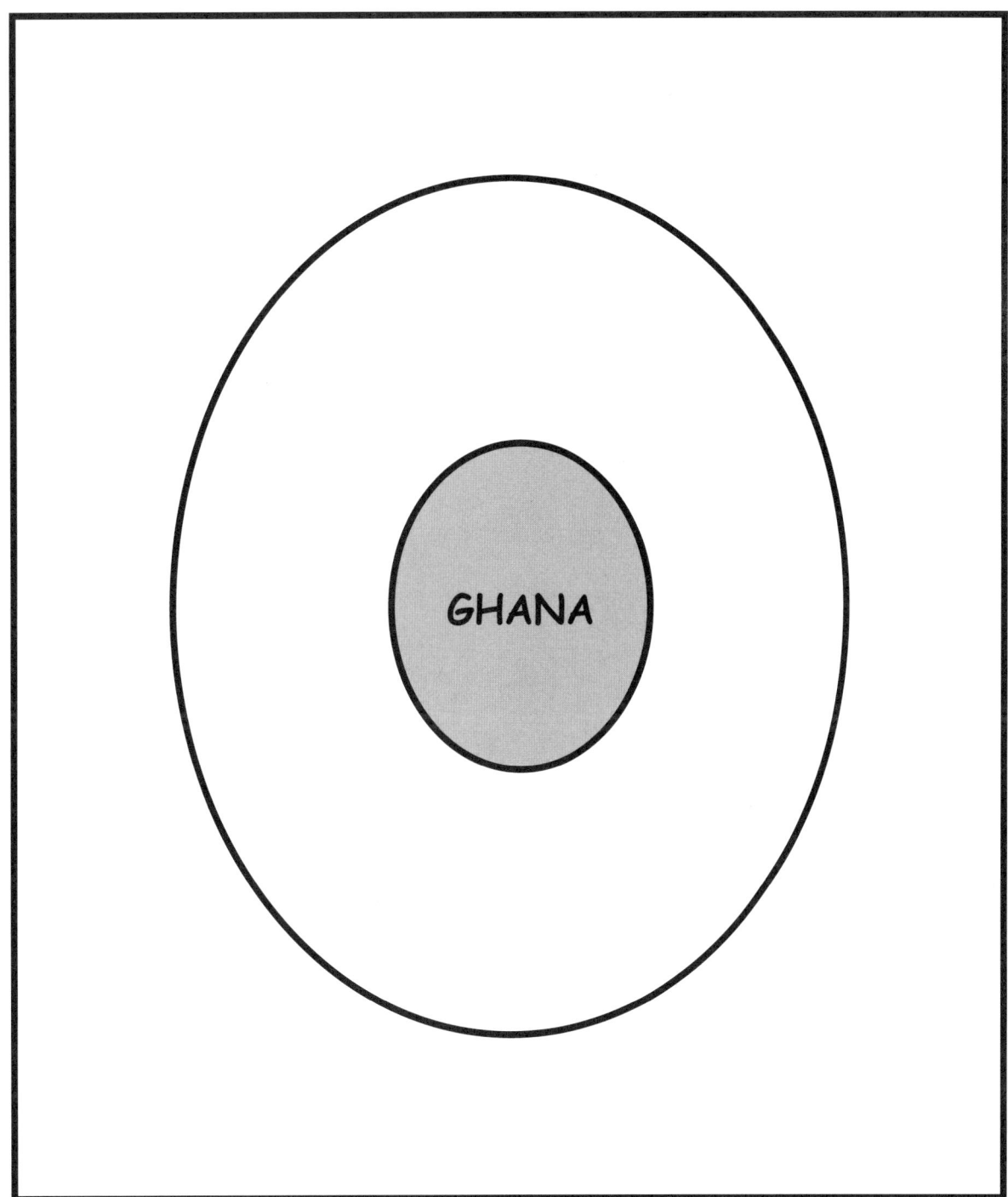

FORCE & MOTION

A RESEARCH-BASED APPROACH TO LEARNING THE PRINCIPLES OF MOTION, CULMINATING IN A STUDENT-LED SYMPOSIUM USING THE SCIENCE BEHIND SPORTS AS A VEHICLE FOR LEARNING.

KAREN FINTER
WEST IRONDEQUOIT CENTRAL SCHOOL DISTRICT
ROCHESTER, NY

OVAL 1: WHAT SHOULD STUDENTS KNOW AND BE ABLE TO DO?

CONTENT STANDARDS & ALIGNMENT

NYS Standards	WI Outcomes	Activities
Analysis, Inquiry & Design: Explanations: The central purpose of scientific inquiry is to develop explanations of natural phenomena in a continuing, creative process.	Employ mathematics in gathering and presenting data and analyzing risk/benefit.	* Calculating Speed & Acceleration (Class Experiments)
STANDARD 4: The Physical Setting		
4.1C Most activities in everyday life involve on form of energy being transformed into another. For example, the chemical energy in gasoline is transformed into mechanical energy in an automobile engine. Energy, in the form of heat, is almost always one of the products of energy transformations.	Design and conduct a demonstration to show how energy is transferred without being destroyed. Identify each type of energy.	Lab: Pulleys; Calculating Mechanical Advantage; Conservation of Energy
4.1e Energy can be considered to be kinetic energy, which is the energy of motion, or potential energy, which depends on position.	Compare and contrast energy of motion and stored energy	Potential and Kinetic Energy Demonstrations & Problems
5.1a The motion of an object is always judged with respect to some other object or point. The idea of absolute motion or rest is misleading.	** *Identify points of reference when describing motion.*	A Walk in the Park Lab
5.1b Its position, direction of motion and speed can describe the motion of an object.	Relate and describe the relationship between the amount of applied force and the overall direction of motion.	Physics of Car Crashes: Videotape & Discussion Table Hockey
5.1c An object's motion is the result of the combined effect of all forces acting on the object. A moving object that is not subjected to a force will continue to move at a constant speed in a straight line. An object at rest will remain at rest.	Design an experiment to test forces due to acceleration and create a graph to represent the motion. Design an experiment to demonstrate the effect of unbalanced forces on an object.	Acceleration Lab Moving Marbles
5.1d Force is directly related to an object's mass and acceleration. The greater the force, the greater the change in motion.	Describe the functions of machines in terms of work and power.	Work & Power Lab Simple Machines Labs
5.1e For every action there is an equal and opposite reaction.	** *Demonstrate Newton's third law.*	Newton's Laws Demonstrations
5.2a Every object exerts gravitational force on every other object. Gravitational force depends on how much mass the objects have, and how far apart they are. Gravity is one of the forces acting on orbiting objects and projectiles.	Relate and describe the relationship between the amount of applied force and the overall direction of motion. (**As it relates to the force of gravity)	Newton's Second Law Lab

NYS Standards	WI Outcomes	Activities
5.2c Machines transfer mechanical energy from one object to another.	...Analyze energy transformations. Design and conduct an experiment to show how energy is transferred without being destroyed.	Moving Marbles Table Hockey
5.2d Friction is a force that opposes motion.	**Compare and contrast helpful vs. harmful friction.*	Table Hockey
5.2e A machine can be made more efficient by reducing friction. Some common ways of reducing friction include lubricating or waxing surfaces.	Describe the functions of machines in terms of work and power.	Work and Power Lab Mechanical Advantage Lab w/ Pulleys Simple Machines Demos
5.2f Machines can change the direction or amount of force, or the distance or speed of force required to do work.	Describe the functions of machines in terms of work and power.	Work and Power Lab Mechanical Advantage Lab w/ Pulleys Simple Machines Demos
5.2g Simple machines include a lever, a pulley, a wheel and axle, and an inclined plane. A complex machine uses a combination of interacting simple machines, e.g., a bicycle.	Describe the functions of machines in terms of work and power.	Work and Power Lab Mechanical Advantage Lab w/ Pulleys Simple Machines Demos

** "Anticipated" gap in outcome/state standards. WI outcomes were written using **national** MST standards, and **then** aligned with NY State.

ESSENTIAL SKILLS

Process Skills Based on NYS Standard 4

General Skills:
1. follow safety procedures in the classroom and laboratory
2. safely and accurately use the following measurement tools:
   - metric ruler
   - stopwatch
   - spring scale
3. Use appropriate units for measured or calculated values
4. recognize and analyze patterns and trends
5. identify cause and effect relationships

Physical Setting Skills:
1. Determine the speed and acceleration of a moving object

KEY CONCEPTS & UNDERSTANDINGS

(ESSENTIAL TO KNOW)

After the completion of this unit, all students will have a deep understanding of Key Ideas 4 & 5. Students will be able to address the bullets under each Key Idea in a comprehensive manner.

4. Energy exists in many forms and when these forms change, energy is conserved.
    a. Describe the sources and identify the transformations of energy observed in everyday life.
    e. Describe the situations that support the principle of conservation of energy.

5. Energy and matter interact through forces that result in changes in motion.
    a. Describe different patterns of motion.
    b. Observe, describe and compare the effects of forces (gravity, electric current and magnetism) on the motion of objects.

Based on the MST Intermediate Level Science Curriculum Guide

> OVAL 2: HOW WILL MY STUDENTS AND I KNOW WHEN THEY ARE SUCCESSFUL?

EVIDENCE OF UNDERSTANDING

Performance Task/Project:
Science Behind Sports: This project involves the analysis of the underlying physics concepts behind a sport or leisure activity. Technical information on the sport will be collected through research, using both printed and electronic resources. After initial research is conducted, students will develop, conduct and analyze an original experiment based on a scientifically sound problem. Finally, research information and experimental results will be communicated throughout the grade level in a student-led symposium.

Homework: Homework usually serves one of three purposes: preparatory, reflective or practice. Depending on the purpose, homework will be either collected or reviewed with the class.

Quizzes:
1. Calculating Speed & Velocity
2. At Snail's Pace: A Quiz on Speed & Acceleration
3. Newton's Laws of Motion

Partner quizzes will be utilized with Quiz #2. Students benefit from working through the problems with someone else, and in effect "teach" one another they're thinking strategies. Another strategy that I employ with some quizzes is the Millionaire approach. Students are give three lifelines: Consult the text, 50/50 or Rephrase the question. Students have the chance to use the lifelines as needed throughout the quiz.

Tests:
As with all units or themes in the 7th or 8th grade level, culminating unit tests are formatted after the 4-part State format. Prior to testing, students are provided review materials (booklets, sessions, practice problems). Accommodations could include allowing students to prepare a "cheat sheet"

of notes, formulas or examples. In the past, students have been allowed to bring in one 3 x 5-index card with information to use while taking the test.

Self/Group Assessment:
As with any group project, it is helpful to hear candidly from students their perceptions about what they contributed to their group, and how their group members also contributed to the effort. After projects are completed, a group assessment guide is given out to team members. Large discrepancies in perceptions are addressed in a group meeting with me. Sometimes, the comments could be connected to point value or percentages of earned points, while at other times, these peer assessments are for informational purposes only.

TASK ANALYSIS

What students will <u>need to know</u> in order to complete task:

- Related vocabulary such as: motion, speed, acceleration, inertia, forces, gravity, centripetal force, centrifugal force, momentum, friction, work, power, kinetic energy, potential energy, conservation of energy, mechanical advantage
- Relationship between distance and time, velocity and time as it relates to determining course of motion
- Effect of gravity on all objects, especially falling objects
- Relationship between mass, velocity and momentum.
- Real-life examples of Newton's Three Laws of Motion
- Relationship between potential and kinetic energy and the conservation of energy
- What friction is, the by-product of friction and ways to increase or reduce it
- How machines make work easier by providing a mechanical advantage
- How energy is constantly converted from one form to another
- How to effectively conduct an independent experiment and data analysis

What students will need to be able to do in order to complete task:
- **Construct and interpret graphs** showing relationships between distance and time in regards to the motion of an object

- Construct and interpret graphs showing relationships between velocity and time in regards to the acceleration of an object
- Given the necessary variables, **calculate** speed, velocity, acceleration, force, work power and mechanical advantage
- Effectively **research** a selected sport
- **Sort** research to identify important information
- **Develop and conduct** a sound experiment involving performance ideals within their selected sport.
- **Organize** research information and experimental results into a meaningful and informational presentation
- **Defend** results of experiment and research findings

COLLEGIAL CONNECTIONS

The implications for connections within this unit are immense. The team structure at Dake allows for collaboration between core subjects (math, science, social studies and English) as well as with a special educator assigned to the team. A teamwide "Quality Paragraph" rubric will be used to assess writing materials as part of the performance task.

Within the subject area, the three 8th grade science teachers will be involved with the unit and the performance task at the same time. The expectations, guidelines and learning experiences are common among the teams.

OVAL 3: WHAT LEARNING EXPERIENCES WILL FACILITATE THEIR SUCCESS?

EQUIPPING STUDENTS

Teaching and Learning Experiences that will Equip Students to Demonstrate Understanding

Standard Alignment:
Students in my classroom utilize an interactive notebook. Within this context, at the start of every unit, the standards for the unit are addressed, as well as the outcomes associated with that standard. Students maintain a copy of these standards within their spiral, and reflect on their progress in meeting the associated outcomes.

** Numbers do not correspond to length of lesson/activity, merely they describe the order of learning experiences.

1. Conduct Unit Anticipation Guide Activity (see attached)
2. Introduce Standards and Outcomes for the Unit
3. Begin Read Aloud: Rocket Boys; Use spiral to reflect on weekly sections
4. A Walk in the Park...Experiment to identify frames of reference, relationship between distance and time
5. Lesson on Speed and Velocity: Calculations & units
6. Interpreting Speed and Velocity Graphs
7. QUIZ 1: Speed and Velocity
8. Moving Marbles...Experiment to determine how acceleration changes as an object travels down a ramp
9. Lesson on Acceleration: calculations and units
10. Interpreting Acceleration Graphs
11. Gravitational Force
12. Acceleration Lab...determining the acceleration due to gravity on falling objects
13. Re-enforcing calculations of acceleration, speed and velocity** Differentiated cubes
14. At Snail's Pace **Partner Quiz
15. Introduce Science of Sports Performance Assessment
16. Students select groups and sport for focus
17. Students develop a timeline of activities and "contract" for completion
18. Lesson on Forces: friction, momentum, centripetal, centrifugal

19. Table Hockey Activity
20. Balanced vs. unbalanced forces
21. Lesson: Newton's Laws of Motion
22. Newton's Second Law Lab: Force = Mass x Acceleration
23. Quiz: Newton's Laws of Motion: Open spiral
24. Watch "Physics of Car Crashes" and complete reflection activity
25. Lesson on: Conservation of energy as it relates to motion
26. Students conduct research for performance assessment
27. Lesson: calculating mechanical advantage
28. Using Pulleys for Mechanical Advantage Lab
29. Review Materials Provided in-class for unit test
30. Rocket Boys Read-aloud completed; Reflection completed in spirals
31. Re-group performance assessment; experimental design
32. Conduct performance-based experiments; generate reports
33. Unit Test: Force & Motion
34. Performance Assessment Wrap-up
35. Performance Assessment Student Symposium: "The Science of Selected Sports..."

DIFFERENTIATION & ACCOMODATIONS

A. Grouping Strategies
- Direct instruction can be accomplished using 10:2 format, with a partner available to Think-Pair-Reflect/Share
- Lab Activities are usually done in a small group (3-4 students/group). Groups may be student selected or teacher selected, depending on the level of difficulty or cooperation needed.
- For research groups, students will have some input as to one other person in their group. The remainder of the group will be selected based on heterogeneous grouping strategies.
- Question/answer cards, word/definition cards or concept/diagram cards can quickly accomplish Pairings. For this unit especially, there are multiple opportunities to work with partners.

B. Vocabulary/Reading Strategies
- Vocabulary terms are addressed using the Frayer model. Students with a wide variety of learning styles can then assimilate the word. By using this model, the definition is looked up, written, re-

formulated and a drawing is created by the student to simulate the word or concept. A "sign" for that word can also be created, to incorporate the kinesthetic learning style.
- Active reading strategies, including symbol-creation, highlighting, and about-point can be used to increase the comprehension of all students.
  - Symbol creation allows students to react to what they have read using a student-generated symbol scheme. For instance, if they have a question about what they read in the first paragraph, they mark a ? on a sticky note or "book-mark" that correlates to the paragraphs on the page. Other symbols can be used to show understanding, ideas, confusion, ease, etc...
  - Highlighting is a strategy that all students need to be taught. It can be especially helpful for the student who is artistic in style, as the color can reinforce memory.
  - About point is a large or small group strategy, where, after students read a selected sentence or passage, they complete the phrase: That passage was about.........and the author's point for writing it was......" The strategy can be modified to include examples, etc...

C. Reflection Strategies
- Within their interactive notebooks, students are given the opportunity to reflect on the work that they have accomplished in class. I am still in the process of developing the notebooks, but I think that a powerful tool to use as a study-guide should be the notebook, where students can go through their work and re-write key concepts or phrases on the margin, color-code or draw other relevant points, or create some other way to "reflect" on what they have accomplished. Using the spiral also provides an excellent way to frame the learning each day, as students can respond to demonstrations, prompts or diagrams in their spirals as a warm-up.

D. Test-taking Strategies
- Quizzes, modeled after the state assessments, can be differentiated as needed. Partner-based quizzes, choice of question or response format, and helper sheets are all tools to use when measuring the students' path to the standards.
- Students may take quiz assessments at different levels (A or B), or with the ability to make up their performance, if it falls below what they had hoped to achieve.

- Tests are modeled after the state assessment in format and questioning style.

E. Performance Task Differentiation Capabilities
- Students are provided choice in partner (at least one group member)
- Students are provided choice in selection of sport
- Students are provided choice in level of attainment
- Students are provided choice in reporting format
- Students are provided with a varying amount of research support & reporting framework.

The Science Behind Sports
Student Packet

Welcome Sports Fans! This is your opportunity to learn all of the "tricks of the trade" about your favorite sport! You and a group will
1. Investigate a selected sport (from an extended list)
2. Relate it to Newton's Three Laws of Motion and other motion concepts
3. Choose a way to publish information
4. Publish It!
5. Set-up Display
6. Finally, present your findings in a school-wide sport symposium!

Feeling a bit overwhelmed? Here is a handy calendar to keep you on task!

Monday	Tuesday	Wednesday	Thursday	Friday
1. Project Intro. 2. Teams Form 3. Topic choices submitted	1. Bibliographies reviewed 2. Topics distributed	In-class research (Library)	In-class research (Computer Lab)	Week 1 Group Summaries Due
1. Select Presentation choice 2. Begin Rough draft & assign roles	1. Continue to fill in information, 2. Design presentation materials	In-class research (Library)	In-class research (Computer Lab)	Week 2 Group Summaries Due

Step 1: Choosing your Partner....

On the slip of paper provided, write the names of two possible partners for this investigation. In order for your choice to be valid, your name must also appear on their paper! Groupings will be based on your input!

Write the name of your FINAL group members here:

_____

_____

_____

Step 2: Choosing your Sport...

From the list provided, rank your top five choices. When asked, supply that information to the whole group. Your final choice will come from those five.

List your top five choices here:

_____

_____

_____

_____

Circle the one that your group receives.

Step 3: Researching....

You and your group are on a quest. You are to find as much information as possible about the mechanics of your selected sport. Each group is to keep a running log of the day's events, as well as a check on the types of information found. To guide you on this quest, here are some questions you should be able to answer as a result of your research. Space after the question has been left for you to record bibliography information. Keep your notes on the note cards as discussed in class. By the way, this list is only a framework! Try to exceed these questions as you explore your interest in the sport.

1. What types of motion does the sport involve? (Circular path, straight line, etc.)	2. What is the role of air resistance or friction in this sport? How are they used? How are they dealt with or reduced?
3. How is momentum used/dealt with in this sport?	4. Identify how Newton's first law relates to the sport. (Objects at rest...)
5. Identify how Newton's second law relates to the sport (Force = mass x acceleration)	6. Identify how Newton's third law relates to the sport (Every action...)
7. What types of equipment are used in this sport?	8. Are there any connections between physics principles and the equipment used? (Like, why do golf balls have dimples?)
9. What speeds are reached in this sport? Acceleration intervals?	10. How is technology used to enhance the sport?

11. What are the energy conversions in this sport?	12. How is energy conserved in this sport?
13. Other	14. Other
15. Other	16. Other

Step 4. Putting It All Together

A. From your research, it will be up to your group to design a show-board, highlighting your findings regarding the 12 questions, as well as any other important information that you may find. The showboard will be shared with class members during the symposium.

B. <u>In addition</u> to the show-board, your group will need to publish your information in one of three ways:

1. Create a webpage, outlining information and containing links to sport-related web-sites.
OR
2. Create a PowerPoint presentation, outlining information in a unique and creative way
OR
3. Create a Picture-Book about the Physics of the sport, including illustrations!

The publications will serve to teach a larger audience about the science behind certain sports. These publications and presentations will be made available to future classes at Dake for research purposes.

Regardless of the choice you make<u>, all publications must:</u>

- Be completed in a professional manner (spelling, grammar, etc...)
- <u>Clearly</u> show the science behind the sport: How do Newton's Laws apply?, What types of forces effect the player?, etc...
- Discuss/model the energy transfers involved within that sport.

Literature Research Rubric

Attributes	Above Standard	Standard	Still A Goal	Points Earned
Research Synthesis	10-9 Make meaning of the information researched by generating original example calculations, illustrations or graphs for use in presentation	8.5-7 Make partial meaning of information researched, try to generate original examples.	6.5-0 Students make little or no meaning of the information researched and cannot use as a tool to develop original examples.	/10
Depth of Research	10-9 Information includes basics as well as an in-depth study of the sport	8.5-7 Information includes the basics and an in-depth study has begun	6.5-0 Information is incomplete and does not include basic information	/10
Diagrams	10-9 At least 3 diagrams are included that increase the understanding of the scientific concept	8.5-7 2 diagrams are included that increase the understanding of the scientific concept	6.5-0 Diagrams are missing or do not aid in the understanding of the concept	/10
Bibliography	10-9 An accurate and extensive bibliography has been developed which includes: at least 2 electronic sources, 2 books and 1 magazine	8.5-7 An accurate and extensive bibliography has been developed which includes: at least 1 electronic source, and 2 books.	6.5-0 Bibliography is incomplete, sources are not referenced or bibliography is missing.	/10

Total: /40

Sympiosium Rubric

Attributes	Above Standard	Standard	Still A Goal	Points Earned
Relationship to Science Concepts	10-9 Information presented clearly shows relationships of: motion, force, acceleration, etc..Players and equipment are addressed.	8.5-7 Information shows relationships of motion, force etc..but may not cover all aspects of the sport or the concept.	6.5-0 Information shows little relationship to science concepts. Aspects of sport are not completely addressed.	/10
Quality of Information	10-9 Information shown in a professional manner, easy to read and understand.	8.5-7 Information shown in a professional manner, may not be easily understood.	6.5-0 Presentation is unprofessional and is not easily understood.	/10
Visuals & Supplementary Materials	10-9 Oral reports include at least 3 computer-generated or handmade visuals. Visuals & supplementals add understanding of presentation.	8.5-7 Oral reports include at least 2 computer-generated or handmade visuals. Visuals & supplementals may/may not add to the understanding of report.	6.5-0 Oral reports did not include computer-generated or handmade visuals.	/10
Presentation	10-9 Group members provide a clear, concise description of sport and relevant connections. Questions are handled in a relevant manner. All members participate	8.5-7 Group members may provide a clear, concise presentation, but relevant connections are weak or lacking. Not all members participate.	6.5-0 Group presentation is uninformative. Not all members participate.	/10

Total: /40

Student Observation Criteria

Your group's effort, cooperation, teamwork and communication will be observed and rated by your teacher on a daily basis. These informal observations will be the basis of your student observation grade. This aspect of your project will be 30/200 points. The criteria are as follows:

Use of Class Time Came to class prepared and equipped. Made effective use of time. Were on task and actively involved in the project.

Team Work Work together as a well-coordinated team. Divide large tasks into smaller pieces for all to contribute. Team members pulled their own share.

Communication/ Leadership: Project leader was assigned, other roles also assigned: technology expert, materials manager, and science expert. Group used high levels of communication with one another and teacher throughout the project.

Publication Criteria

Web Pages:
- Have at least 3 links to other sites regarding sports
- Be at least 2 web-pages long
- Summarize your findings and scientific connections
- Contain at least 2 diagrams, clip-art, data table, or other visual
- Be creative, neat, and ready to up-load to the Dake Website.

Picture Books:
- Are at least 10 content pages in length
- Include title page, dedication, and cover
- Contain findings and scientific information
- Contain at least 5 diagrams, clip-art, data tables, or other visuals.

PowerPoint Presentations:
- Are at least 10 slides in length
- Contain findings and scientific connections
- Contain at least 2 diagrams, clip-art, data tables, or other visuals.
- Contain one video clip with sound bites.
- Be creative, neat, and ready to upload onto the Dake Website.

About the Author

Paula Rutherford is the author of four books, **Instruction for All Students**, **Leading the Learning: A Field Guide for Supervision and Evaluation**, **The 21st Century Mentor's Handbook**, and **Why Didn't I Learn This in College?** She writes an e-newsletter titled: **Mentoring in the 21st Century**®.

Paula is president of Just ASK Publications & Professional Development, established in 1989 and based in Alexandria, Virginia. She works extensively with districts as they engage in long-term systemic work to align processes such as hiring, induction, professional development, school improvement plans, and supervision and evaluation. She also leads **Mentoring in the 21st Century**® **Institutes** across the country and has developed a comprehensive **Mentoring in the 21st Century**® **Resource Kit** so that districts can replicate the Just ASK institutes and provide extensive follow-up support for mentors. Paula is committed to building in-house capacity and has developed a **New Teacher Professional Development Resource Kit** and a Certified Local Trainer (CLT) program based on **Instruction for All Students**, **Leading the Learning**, and **Why Didn't I Learn This in College?**

In addition to her extensive work as a consultant and trainer, Paula's professional experience includes work in regular education K-12 as a teacher of high school history and social sciences, physical education, Spanish, and kindergarten, as well as a special education teacher, coordinator of special education programs, school administrator at the middle school and high school levels, and as a central office staff development specialist.

She can be reached at paula@justaskpublications.com.

Books

Why Didn't I Learn This in College?
by Paula Rutherford

Over 300,000 copies of the first edition are in the hands of new teachers and their mentors worldwide. This new edition includes updated tools and procedures for teaching and learning in the 21st century. Even veteran teachers say that they find the ideas and strategies here invaluable. It is based on the construct that the best management program is a good instructional program. If student learning is our goal, we want to shift our focus from control and compliance to creating positive learning-centered environments. A CD-ROM of templates is included.

$29.95   ISBN 978-0-9797280-1-3   330 pages   Order# 11002

Instruction for All Students
by Paula Rutherford

The second edition of this popular book is updated to reflect current research about best practice in teaching and learning in standards-based classrooms. In addition to resources for actively engaging students and multiple approaches to lesson and unit design, this text includes information on technology integration, formative assessment, 21st century thinking skills that promote rigor and relevance, and formats for job-embedded learning. A CD-ROM of templates is included.

$34.95   ISBN 978-0-9777796-8-0   298 pages   Order# 11027

Instruction for All Students Facilitator's Handbook
by Paula Rutherford

This 160-page facilitator's handbook is designed to help educators structure their reading and use of the strategies presented in the book *Instruction for All Students*. It can be used for book clubs, study groups, and in team, department, and faculty meetings. The learning experiences are interactive and action-oriented. The handbook is written with the expectation that group participants will use what they study, and come to the next session ready to share and discuss how they used what they learned. A CD-ROM of templates is included.

$24.95   ISBN 978-0-9797280-2-0   160 pages   Order# 11043

The 21st Century Mentor's Handbook
by Paula Rutherford

The 21st Century Mentor's Handbook is cross-referenced to *Why Didn't I Learn This in College?* and *Instruction for All Students*. Mentors find it an indispensable tool in planning their interactions with new teachers. This handbook provides a multitude of resources including a mentoring calendar, needs assessments, tools for goal setting and reflection, instructional design templates, guidelines for observation and coaching, and field tested ways to deal with the potential problems of novice teachers. A CD-ROM of templates is included.

$34.95   ISBN 978-0-9663336-6-4   380 pages   Order# 11003

Just ASK | www.justaskpublications.com | Phone: 800-940-5434 | Fax: 703-535-8502

Books

Meeting the Needs of Diverse Learners
by Paula Rutherford

Meeting the Needs of Diverse Learners is designed to help teachers build skillfulness in recognizing, respecting, and responding to the needs of the wide range of students in today's classrooms. This book provides an array of strategies for use with second language learners, special needs students, accelerated learners, and proposes that those strategies are, in fact, productive strategies for all students. A CD-ROM of templates is included.

$34.95   ISBN 978-0-9777796-9-7   Order# 11033

Available Summer 2009

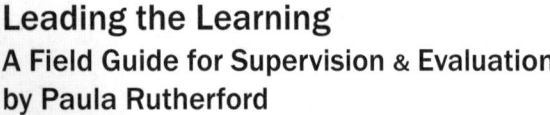

Leading the Learning
A Field Guide for Supervision & Evaluation
by Paula Rutherford

This field guide explores the contexts in which educational leaders work to ensure that there is a fully qualified and satisfied teacher in each classroom. It provides in-depth information on best practices to notice, suggestions to make, and reflective questions to ask in the six areas of teacher performance. Strategies for gathering and analyzing data about teaching and learning from multiple sources are accompanied by clearly explained feedback options. A CD-ROM of templates is included.

$34.95   ISBN 978-0-9663336-7-1   300 pages   Order# 11005
$59.95 3-Ring Binder   ISBN 978-0-9663336-3-3   300 pages   Order# 11004

Results-Based Professional Development Models
edited by Brenda Kaylor

This extraordinary resource was developed by the Office of Professional Development, St. Vrain Valley Public School District, Longmont, Colorado. The text provides all the tools professional developers need to introduce and implement five models: coaching/mentoring, independent study, inquiry, process, and training. The use of these models supports NSDC's purpose of ensuring that every educator engages in effective professional development every day so every student achieves.

$70.00 3-Ring Binder   ISBN 978-0-9777796-5-9   114 pages   Order# 11011

Standards-Based Classroom Operator's Manual
designed by Centennial BOCES, Longmont, Colorado

This resource provides facilitator notes and timelines for use by professional developers as they help teachers move from being standards-referenced to standards-based. It also includes an extensive array of copy-ready graphic organizers and templates for teacher use in designing and implementing standards-based lessons in their classrooms. Elementary, middle, and high school exemplars of the templates are provided. These tools are perfect for collaborative use in team and department meetings.

$45.00   ISBN 978-0-9777796-6-6   149 pages   Order# 11012

Just ASK | www.justaskpublications.com | Phone: 800-940-5434 | Fax: 703-535-8502

Resource Kits

New Teacher Professional Development Kit

Professional development opportunities designed to address the needs of new teachers are an essential component of induction programs. **The New Teacher Professional Development (NTPD) Kit** provides the resources you need to design a comprehensive new teacher professional development program for your school or district.

The kit includes:

- ☑ *New Teacher Professional Development Facilitator's Handbook* in hard copy and on CD-ROM (available only with purchase of the kit)
- ☑ *New Teacher Professional Development Participant's Manual* in hard copy and on CD-ROM (available only with purchase of the kit)
- ☑ A copy of *Why Didn't I Learn This in College?* with CD-ROM of tools
- ☑ A copy of *Strategies in Action: A Collection of Classroom Applications*
- ☑ A copy of *The 21st Century Mentor's Handbook* with CD-ROM of tools
- ☑ A copy of *Instruction for All Students* with CD-ROM of tools
- ☑ A selection of DVDs including classroom exemplars of best practice
- ☑ **CD-ROM of Visual Tools** (an expanded collection of JPEG and PDF files)
- ☑ *Why Didn't I Learn This in College?* **Scavenger Hunt Cards**
- ☑ **What Do You Do When... Cards for New Teachers**

$795.00   Order# 11046

The kit features options for one day or multi-day orientation sessions and ongoing follow-up support sessions for novice teachers, alternative certification teachers, and teachers new to the district. The formats and learning experiences detailed in the *NTPD Facilitator's Handbook* have been field-tested in districts, large and small, across the country.

> The kit is designed to be used with the text *Why Didn't I Learn This in College?* The focus questions are:
> - What is a learning-centered environment and how do I create such an environment?
> - How do I translate "beginning with the end in mind" into planning and pacing for the year, the unit, and the lesson?
> - What are systems, procedures, and routines for organizing my professional and instructional materials, the learners, and the classroom learning environment?

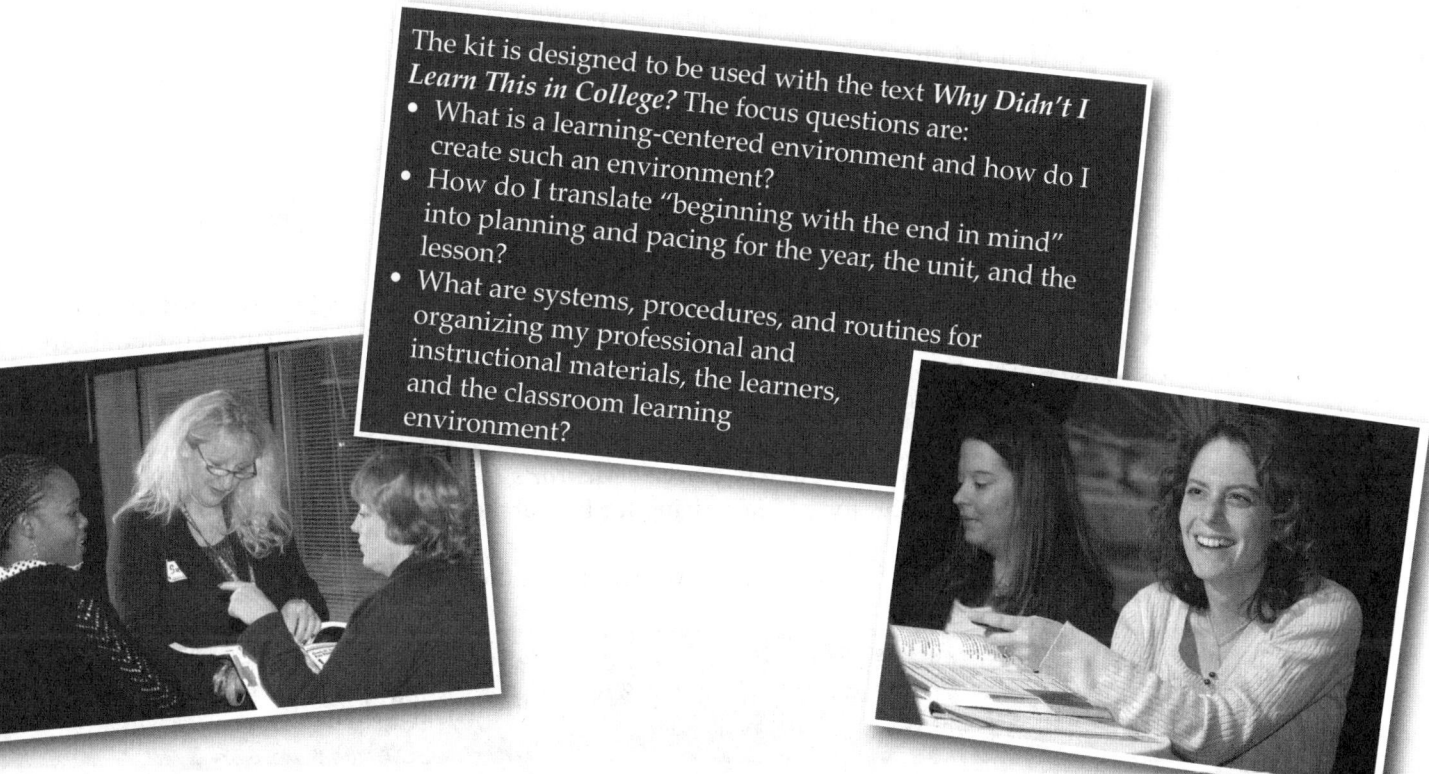

Just ASK | www.justaskpublications.com | Phone: 800-940-5434 | Fax: 703-535-8502

Resource Kits

Mentoring in the 21st Century® Resource Kit

The **Mentoring in the 21st Century® Resource Kit** provides the tools you need to design and implement a comprehensive mentor training program for your school or district. It offers **over 30 hours** of professional development learning exercises that have been field-tested in our national **Mentoring in the 21st Century® Institutes** and on-site in schools and districts like yours.

A Complete Mentor Training Program

$985.00   Order# 11028

The kit includes:

- ☑ *Mentoring in the 21st Century® Facilitator's Handbook* in hard copy and on CD-ROM (available only with purchase of the kit)
- ☑ *Mentoring in the 21st Century® Participant's Manual* in hard copy and on CD-ROM (available only with purchase of the kit)
- ☑ **CD-ROM of Visual Tools** (an expanded collection of JPEG and PDF files)
- ☑ **Collegial Conversations DVD** with viewing guide (See page 4 for details.)
- ☑ **What Do You Do When... Cards** (See page 10 for details.)
- ☑ **Scavenger Hunt Cards** (See page 10 for details.)
- ☑ A collection of DVDs and videos
- ☑ A set of nine 18" x 24" posters
- ☑ A copy of *The 21st Century Mentor's Handbook*, *Why Didn't I Learn This in College?* and *Instruction for All Students* by Paula Rutherford

The 180-page *Mentoring in the 21st Century® Facilitator's Handbook* includes everything you need to design half-day, full-day, and multiple-day workshops, and follow-up support sessions. All participant materials are included on the CD-ROM. This handbook provides explicit directions on how to use the components of the resource kit and is available only with purchase of the **Mentoring in the 21st Century® Resource Kit**.

Each workshop participant needs a copy of *The 21st Century Mentor's Handbook* and a copy of *Why Didn't I Learn This in College?* Contact Just ASK for special pricing for kit purchasers.

Participant's Manuals can be printed from the CD-ROM included in the kit or ordered from Just ASK.

ASK Group consultants are available to lead a mentoring institute in your district; they can model use of the resource kit and help you build in-house capacity.

Just ASK | www.justaskpublications.com | Phone: 800-940-5434 | Fax: 703-535-8502

Ordering Information

Books	Order #	Price
Instruction for All Students	11027	$ 34.95
Instruction for All Students Facilitator's Handbook	11043	$ 24.95
Leading the Learning (3-ring binder)	11004	$ 59.95
Leading the Learning (bound)	11005	$ 34.95
Meeting the Needs of Diverse Learners	11033	$ 34.95
Results-Based Professional Development Models	11011	$ 70.00
Standards-Based Classroom Operator's Manual	11012	$ 45.00
The 21st Century Mentor's Handbook	11003	$ 34.95
Why Didn't I Learn This in College? Second Edition	11002	$ 29.95
Why Didn't I Learn This in College? and The 21st Century Mentor's Handbook Save 20%	11029	$ 50.00

Videos and DVDs	Order #	Price
Collegial Conversations DVD	11031	$ 295.00
Common Ground Video and Facilitator's Guide CD-ROM	11020	$ 30.00
Helping New Teachers Succeed DVD	11021	$ 60.00
Lesson Collection: Biology Visual Learning Tools (ASCD) DVD	11026	$ 95.00
Lesson Collection: HS Geometry Surface Area and Volume (ASCD) DVD	11034	$ 95.00
Lesson Collection: HS Reciprocal Teaching (ASCD) DVD	11035	$ 95.00
Lesson Collection: Primary Math (ASCD) DVD	11025	$ 95.00
Points to Ponder DVD	11016	$ 29.95
Principles in Action DVD	11019	$ 19.95
Success Factors in a Standards-Based Classroom DVD	11017	$ 75.00

Other Products	Order #	Price
Mentoring in the 21st Century® Resource Kit	11028	$ 985.00
New Teacher Professional Development Resource Kit	11046	$ 795.00
Poster Pack	11006	$ 16.95
Visual Tools: The Complete Collecton CD-ROM	11041	$ 375.00
Visual Tools: Instruction for All Students CD-ROM	11036	$ 100.00
Visual Tools: Leading the Learning CD-ROM	11039	$ 100.00
Visual Tools: The 21st Century Mentor's Handbook CD-ROM	11038	$ 100.00
Visual Tools: Why Didn't I Learn This in College?® CD-ROM	11037	$ 100.00
What Do You Do When... Cards (for mentors and administrators)	11032	$ 49.95
Scavenger Hunt Cards: Instruction for All Students	11044	$ 10.00
Scavenger Hunt Cards: Why Didn't I Learn This in College?	11045	$ 10.00

Prices subject to change without notice

To Order

Call
800-940-5434

Fax
703-535-8502

Online
www.justaskpublications.com

Mail
2214 King Street, Alexandria, VA 22301

Order Form

Just ASK Publications & Professional Development

Ship To

Name _____
Title _____
School/District _____
_____
Address _____
City_____ State_____ ZIP_____
Email _____
Telephone _____
Fax _____

Bill To (If different)

Name _____
Title _____
School/District _____
_____
Address _____
City_____ State_____ ZIP_____
Email _____
Telephone _____
Fax _____

Order #	Title	Quantity	Unit Price	Total Price

Please attach a sheet of paper for additional products ordered

Subtotal _____

Shipping and Handling
$6 S&H minimum per order
15% on orders under 10 units, 10% on orders 10 units and more
$49 S&H for each resource kit

TOTAL _____

Contact us for quantity discounts and special offers
Call 800-940-5434

Payment Method (Select One)

☐ Check (Please make checks or purchase orders payable to Just ASK Publications)

☐ Purchase Order   Purchase Order Number _____

☐ Credit Card   ☐ Visa   ☐ MasterCard   ☐ AMEX

Name as it appears on the card _____
Credit Card # _____
Expiration Date ☐☐ / ☐☐
                 Month   Year

☐ Check here to receive information about Just ASK workshops, institutes, and train-the-trainer opportunities.

Mail or Fax to:
Just ASK Publications
2214 King Street
Alexandria, VA 22301
Fax: 703-535-8502

Instruction for All Students Facilitator's Handbook